GROWING YOUNG
CHURCHES

GROWING YOUNG CHURCHES

CHURCHES

How to Advance Indigenous
Churches Today

by

MELVIN L. HODGES

MOODY PRESS

CHICAGO

Previously published as
On the Mission Field

Revised and enlarged

Copyright © 1970 by
THE MOODY BIBLE INSTITUTE
OF CHICAGO

Printed in the United States of America

CONTENTS

5

"I will build my church; and the gates of hell shall not prevail against it."

—*Jesus in Matthew 16:18*

"The things that thou hast heard of me among many witnesses, the same commit thou to faithful men, who shall be able to teach others also."

—*Paul in II Timothy 2:2*

FOREWORD

Protestant missions are passing through a time of extreme confusion. Goals that were once unquestioned are being discarded. The whole philosophy of evangelical missions is brought into question, and many are taking the viewpoint that the missionary goals and philosophy of the last generation are no longer applicable to the present world situation. Certain churches are no longer sending out "missionaries" but "fraternal workers." With some, evangelism has come to mean social action. We are told that God is working in history, and that while the church is one means that He is using to accomplish His purposes, it is not the only means. The church at home and abroad is urged to identify itself with the social and economic revolution that is taking place and to lose its own identity as a separate people in the hope of renewing society and bringing in the kingdom on a broader basis than would be possible through old-fashioned evangelism.

It is not the author's purpose to enter into a discussion of these questions. We do recognize that we are ministering in a changed world. Transportation and communication have brought the different parts of the world closer together. The disappearance of colonialism and the emergence of new nations have changed the political picture. A missionary enterprise identified with colonialism or paternalism is out of the question. The discoveries of science have changed man's concept of the universe in which he lives. Yet, while all of these exteriors have changed, the heart of man remains the same. We firmly believe that the gospel of Christ is by nature relevant to the twentieth century. What must change are the human methods and philosophies which may have been linked to the past in our missionary effort. This we must insist on. But, in essence, we believe that the New Testament program of church building is God's program for this day also. The adequacy of this position will not be discussed in the following chapters. We accept as basic to our position the biblical concept of missions as set forth in the Acts of the Apostles.

The Spirit of God is still moving in the earth. The possibilities are greater than ever before. The challenge is to the faith of God's messengers. God will accomplish His purpose through men who are wholly dedicated to that purpose and to the fulfilling of the will of God in their own lives.

PREFACE

The author has been gratified to observe the wide acceptance of the book "The Indigenous Church" and of its companion edition "On the Mission Field—The Indigenous Church" since it was first published in 1953. It is being employed as a textbook or as required reading in various seminaries and Bible institutes, both in the United States and abroad.

Missionaries of many different societies have expressed appreciation for the help received. It has enjoyed a ministry far beyond the expectation of the author, who wrote it primarily as a guide and encouragement of his fellow missionaries working with his own board. That God has been pleased to give it a wider ministry, is reason for sincere gratitude to God.

There are no basic changes in this revised edition. Some statistics have been updated and a limited amount of new material has been added, particularly under the chapter "Developing Leadership," where the major portions of a paper "Training the Worker" have been included.

We trust that this revised edition will continue to enjoy the appreciation of our missionary colaborers and be used by God to the furtherance of His kingdom.

1

THE GOAL OF MISSIONS—
A NEW TESTAMENT CHURCH

Today there are more Christian missionaries working in more countries of the world than at any previous period in the history of the church. They are also engaged in more diverse activities. Along with the evangelistic and church-planting ministries are those auxiliary activities of reducing languages to written form, the translating of the Scriptures and training of national pastors and evangelists. There are also a host of other activities not directly related to the evangelistic, church-planting ministry, which include the establishing of hospitals and secular schools, agricultural projects and industrial schools.

It would be logical to suppose that all the different aspects of the outreach of the church in foreign lands would be united by a common goal. Yet, what a variety of answers would be evoked were we to ask missionaries of the Christian faith throughout the world to define their goal! Some might reply that they are endeavoring to Christianize people and better the social conditions so that everyone will be happier and healthier. Others might answer that their purpose is to save souls, and still others to witness to every creature so that Christ's return will be hastened. All of these are worthy objectives, but none is really adequate. Our ultimate goal and the means which we employ to reach the goal are intricately related. If

11

our goal is not clearly defined we may err in the choice
of methods employed and fail to realize the true fruit
of our labors.

Jesus announced His purpose: "I will build my
church." The Apostle Paul states that Jesus loved the
church and gave Himself for it. He himself throughout his epistles describes his own labors as being for the
sake of the church. We can have no better goal than
the one set forth in the New Testament. We would
therefore define our objective in this way: We desire
to establish in the country of our labors a strong church
patterned after the New Testament example. Further,
we believe that in order to have a New Testament
church, we must follow New Testament methods.

The following illustration will emphasize the importance of a well-defined goal. Some years ago certain missionaries were sent to the foreign field by a
group interested primarily in giving the Christian witness to all the earth. They based their objective and
methods on the statement that Jesus had made that
this gospel must be preached to all nations for a witness. Desiring to hasten the return of the Lord and
realizing that the Great Commission must be fulfilled
before that time, they decided that the missionary
should not tarry in any one place for an extended time
but rather push on from city to city and give each
place the gospel witness. Little effort was made to
conserve the results. The converts were not formed
into churches nor given the teaching necessary for them
to carry on in church life. As a consequence, after
years of effort and laborious toil, very little permanent
results of their labor remained. They had preached
over a wide area but churches had not been established.
They had failed to take into consideration, that though
evangelism is important, the ultimate objective of
evangelism is the calling out of a people for the Lord
Jesus Christ. The church itself is God's agent for
evangelism. Later on this missionary group restudied
the situation and changed its methods to conform to

the long-range objective of the establishing of the church of Jesus Christ.

When the social betterment of the populace has been the principal objective of a mission, the tendency usually has been toward developing institutions such as schools, hospitals and agricultural projects. These are all worthy projects and the social betterment of a populace is the desire of every Christian. However, according to the New Testament plan these are by-products rather than the heart of the missionary program. When we fail to see this, we build strong institutions but usually the church itself remains weak. Our observation leads us to believe that when the emphasis is primarily on this type of work, the church is left unprepared to meet a crisis, such as a Communist invasion of the country, which forces the withdrawal of foreign funds and personnel. Left without the crutches of foreign aid, on which she has long been accustomed to depend, she cannot stand alone, and the institutions themselves have succumbed to the enemy. It is the indigenous New Testament church that has been better able to survive under such conditions.

CHARACTERISTICS OF THE NEW TESTAMENT CHURCH

Let us examine the elements in this New Testament church that we propose to establish. A careful study of the book of Acts and the Epistles reveals the methods employed by the apostles, and particularly by the Apostle Paul, the model missionary, as he went forth and preached the gospel to the Jew and to the Gentile. After preaching the gospel in a city, the converts were brought together in a convenient meeting place, often the home of a believer, and other times in any public location that might be available to them, such as a synagogue or a school. These groups of believers would meet together at regular intervals for worship and instruction in Christian doctrine and conduct. Elders and deacons were chosen from among the number to provide the necessary leadership and ministry as they

witnessed to their townspeople and the surrounding
area. For example, Paul was in Thessalonica only a
few weeks, yet he left a church established in that
place. He labored in Ephesus for two years, teaching
in the school of Tyrannus. As a result, all the province
of Asia in Asia Minor heard the Word of the Lord.
His farewell discourse to the Ephesian elders is a
classic on the relationship of a missionary to the
church which he has founded (see Acts 19-20). The
apostle stayed a limited time in one area but he left
behind him a church that could govern itself; that
could finance its own expenses and that extended the
gospel throughout the region. Paul evidently made no
appeals for workers from Jerusalem or Antioch to fill
the pastorates of the churches which he raised up.
And there is no financial appeal made either to Antioch
or Jerusalem for support for workers or for the erection
of church buildings as far as the record shows. Rather,
we find the apostle taking up offerings among these
new missionary churches to help the saints of the
mother church in Jerusalem when that region was
stricken with famine. What a commentary on the
effectiveness of the New Testament methods; how far
we have drifted from that ideal in our present procedure!

The New Testament church then was first, self-
propagating; that is, it had within it sufficient vitality
so that it could extend itself throughout the region and
neighboring regions by its own efforts. It produced
its own workers and the work was spread abroad by
the effort of the Christians themselves. Second, it was
self-governing; that is, it was governed by men who
were raised up by the Holy Spirit from among the converts in the locality. Third, it was self-supporting; it
did not depend on foreign money in order to meet the
expenses of the work.

In view of the fact that the New Testament churches
were not dependent on workers or funds from a foreign
field but were self-sufficient as local units, what could

be said of a church today which must depend upon such foreign help in order to continue to exist? We have known of churches on a mission field which have been established for more than twenty years, with fairly large congregations, which are still unable to support their own pastors. We have heard of a church which after several decades of existence, appealed to the mission board for a new missionary pastor when the retiring pastor was forced to leave the work because of the infirmities of old age. It seems evident that a church that must follow such a procedure is far from the New Testament pattern.

Let us ask ourselves a more searching question. In what condition would we find our work if the mission, because of some emergency, found it necessary to call home its missionaries and cut off funds for the support of our work? Would it be a mortal blow to our church or would our church be able to survive? This is not an idle question since in recent years mission fields have been closed to the missionary for one reason or another. Foreign funds have been withdrawn. The church must be built in such a way that the gates of hell shall not prevail against her. In one field the sponsoring mission passed through a financial crisis and was forced to radically cut funds going to the support of pastors. As a result, pastors failed to find means of support and they left their churches and took secular employment. Abandoned chapels and scattered congregations were the result. It is difficult to escape the conclusion that there was something fundamentally wrong in the life of that church. Surely God does not intend for the church in any country to be so dependent upon a sponsoring foreign mission that when its help is removed the young church sickens and dies.

THE GOAL IS OBTAINABLE

It is possible to obtain the ideal of a church patterned after the New Testament model. This is possible because the gospel has not changed. We serve the same God and His Holy Spirit is with us as He was with the church in the New Testament times. We do not propose to introduce a new pattern or system. We desire simply to return to the New Testament pattern and see a church founded that will bear the characteristics of the apostolic model. We believe that this is possible because the gospel is universal and adaptable to every climate and race, and to every social and economic level. New Testament preaching and practice will produce a New Testament church in any place where the gospel is preached. People of other lands can be converted and empowered by the Holy Spirit to carry on the work of the church equally as well as Americans or Europeans. The gospel has been designed by God Himself, so it fills the need of the African, the Chinese, or the Indian. As a result, there is no place on earth where, if the gospel seed be properly planted, it will not produce an indigenous church. The Holy Spirit can work in one country as well as in another. To proceed on the assumption that the infant church in any land must always be cared for and provided for by the mother mission is an unconscious insult to the people that we endeavor to serve, and is evidence of lack of faith in God and in the power of His gospel.

2

THE NEW TESTAMENT CHURCH—
A RESPONSIBLE CHURCH

We have seen that the New Testament church is a powerful, vital organism with power not only to maintain itself, but to expand and extend itself throughout the country where it has been planted. Yet, we are brought face to face with the fact that too often the churches planted by missionaries on foreign fields are not that kind of church. Why the difference? In some places missionaries have labored for fifty years and still the local congregation is unable to carry on alone. Why is it that after ten, fifteen or twenty years of missionary effort in a given area, we must still appeal to the home churches for additional funds and workers?

One missionary writes as follows:

> Why, today, do we have still a weak church organization that after years of growth cannot yet stand alone? Why has this church, after being organized as a Field Council for more than twenty years, not been able to produce the type of national leadership necessary to develop, sustain and consolidate gains made during periods of revival outpourings? After studying this question for the past ten years, we have come to the conclusion that our problem lies in the *failure to work for an indigenous church*. Unless a church can be taught the necessity of shouldering its own burden and facing its own problems it cannot be expected to develop even with the aid of periodic revival outpourings.

WHY THE WEAKNESSES IN THE NATIONAL CHURCH?

Another, a missionary secretary, analyzes the problem and places the blame directly at the door of the mission and the missionary:

Here is a missionary agency sincerely devoted to assuming a creditable share in world evangelism. Missionary candidates are available. Funds are also available for developing the field in question. Land is purchased, and extensive mission buildings erected; missionary homes, churches, schools, hospitals, dormitories, dispensaries, etc., begin to appear. Workmen are hired, provision is made for maintenance of the youth who enter the various schools. When native workers have been trained, they are placed on salary from funds available to the mission from its home office across the seas. The missionary, whose time and energies are fully occupied with the business management of the vast community, anticipates that here will probably be his home for years to come, so he provides for those extras which make the plan comfortable and convenient.

He is the undisputed master over this establishment. Funds for workmen, for native teachers and preachers flow through his hands. He hires or dismisses, at will. If a native church springs up, it is under his direct supervision. He feels impelled to remain as director of this, his sphere of influence and operations, as long as he remains a missionary. When on furlough, he describes the progress made, the buildings erected, and institutions operating; the number of workers and Bible women employed, the number of teachers and scholars in the schools. He presents pictures of the whole project. He may even mention that beyond are other towns and tribes needing the gospel, and may make an appeal for additional missionaries.

After fifteen to twenty years of this type of work, he may wonder why the native church does not show some signs of standing on its own feet. The workers do not manifest any initiative. The people do not show any concern for the salvation of their neighbors, nor manifest a willingness to assume financial responsibility for any phase of the mission work. He realizes that his removal from the oversight of the mission would practically bring the whole project to a standstill, unless another missionary took over.

What is the reason for this? Simply the plan he has followed. He has treated the people like irresponsible children. He has led them, thought for them, relieved them of all financial responsibility for years. He has unintentionally robbed them of those practical processes which develop strong characters in any walk of life, whether in Canada or China, whether white or yellow-skinned.

Actually, he has founded a sort of spiritual hospital, over which he must be chief nurse as long as it remains. His life work has become a liability instead of an asset. He has sown his leadership and domination and provision of every need, and he has reaped the servitude and malnutrition of a community of undeveloped spiritual children. How difficult to avoid this result in a mission that runs predominantly to institutional development!

Here is the key to the problem: As missionaries, we have too often trained the converts in dependence upon us, rather than in *responsibility*. It may be because we have an overprotectiveness for our converts; it may be that unconsciously we desire to be the head and have people look to us as the indispensable man; it may stem from our lack of faith in the Holy Spirit to do His work in maturing the converts. But for whatever reason, the fact remains that weak churches are often the product of the missionaries' wrong approach to their task. How we long to see vigorous converts who will testify fearlessly to their neighbors! How much the spirit of dedication and sacrifice is needed in order that true leadership will develop! There is one "pearl of great price" in building the church, and that is *a sense of responsibility* on the part of the converts. With it, other things being equal, the church will prosper. Without it, although we bolster the church with a thousand foreign props, in the end it will succumb to the inertia and resistance of the world around. Only

God can produce this sense of responsibility, but the way in which the missionary approaches his task will open or close the door of possibility to this vigorous aspect of Christian living. Here are some things that the missionary must watch:

First, the missionary should have a clear concept of his own work as a missionary and of his proper relationship to the converts. He must understand the transitory aspect of the missionary's ministry in any one area. It has been aptly compared to the scaffolding used in the erection of a building. What would one think of a carpenter if he had to leave the scaffolding up so that the building would not fall down! A missionary may center the work too completely in his own person, in the money that he brings to the work and in his own abilities. He becomes the indispensable man. The nationals learn to depend on him for everything. Consequently they do not develop initiative and the work never reaches the stage where it can be left without missionary supervision. The successful missionary is one who has done his work so well that he is no longer needed in that area. He can leave the work to his converts. "A modern missionary . . . is not intended to be a permanent factor in the life of an alien people. His work is to make Christ the permanent factor, and himself to pass on to other pioneer tasks as quickly as he may. Institutions which tie the foreigner down to permanent work are intrinsically dangerous expedients."[1] The true measure of success is not that which the missionary accomplishes while on the field, but the work that still stands after he has gone.

Is the Mission the Center?

Second, one hindrance may be that the work has been centered in the mission station rather than in the local church. God does not send missionaries out to

[1]Alexander McLeish, "The Effective Missionary," in Sidney J. W. Clark, *The Indigenous Church*, p. 6.

build mission stations, but to build the church. The modern missionary should free himself from the "mission compound" psychology of the past generation. Of course the missionary must have a residence, but the church should be located apart, in the village or city, not on the "compound," and the activities of the converts should center around the church. Workers should be sent out to outstations by the church, and these should be considered as branches of the church rather than of the mission station.

Too Many Missionaries?

Third, the development of the indigenous church may be hindered by a disproportionate number of missionaries in the area. In order to develop the ability and ministry of the nationals, a missionary should never hold a position which a national is able to fill. When there are too many missionaries in proportion to the number of national workers, the tendency is to let the missionaries fill all the important posts. Thus the nationals are not given proper resronsibilities and so fail to develop. Missionary personnel should be so allocated that the missionary will be performing a task that would be left undone if he were not there, and under circumstances that will require him to make use of the nationals in order to meet the demands of the work.

American Methods?

A fourth reason for the failure to produce an indigenous church may be found in the missionary's failure to adapt himself to native psychology and methods. An understandable but excessive fondness for the "American way" may make him feel that American methods are the only right methods. The work must be administered according to the American plan, the Bible school patterned after the Bible school program in the United States. Even the chapel must be built according to the American idea of architecture. The nationals find it difficult to fit into this foreign pattern. Therefore, year after year, the missionary continues the administration according to his own ideas, and the indigenous church does not develop.

Too Much Foreign Money?

Fifth, a frequent hindrance to the development of the indigenous church has been the introduction of foreign funds into the structure of the work, with the result that the church depends on foreign aid for its support and advancement. This weakens the spiritual and moral fiber of the church, kills the initiative of the converts and dulls their sense of responsibility.

Lack of Faith?

Sixth, the missionary may fail to exercise a vigorous faith in God for the development of the spiritual capabilities of his converts. Like a tropical plant in a northern climate, the convert may be placed in a spiritual greenhouse. Sometimes he is separated from his own people and brought to live on the mission compound so he will not slip back into heathenism. The missionary may hesitate to place responsibility upon the shoulders of young converts for fear that they will become discouraged. Perhaps he does not teach them to tithe. Sometimes he fails to take advantage of the new convert's enthusiasm to witness, or has been afraid to allow God-called men to launch out into the ministry, for fear that they would fall into sin. A missionary once said that we could not expect the church on the mission field to take upon itself the ministry of intercession—the converts were too young and inexperienced to understand it!

Not a Dependent Church

We must found a truly indigenous church on the mission field because the church of Jesus Christ in China, in Latin America or in Africa, is not, or should not be, a branch of the church in America. It must be a church in its own right. We should plant the gospel seed and cultivate it in such a way that it will produce the Chinese or the African church. We must train the national church in independence rather than dependence. A church that must depend on foreigners for its workers, that must call for additional missionaries to extend the work, that must plead for foreign funds in order to keep going, is not an indigenous church. It is a hothouse plant that must have artificial atmosphere and receive special care in order to keep alive. When we find ourselves in a situation like this, let us examine the type of work that we are doing. Let us ascertain why we are building a work that cannot progress without artificial help. Surely the weak thing we have produced is not what Jesus meant when He said, "I will build my church; and the gates of hell shall not prevail against it."

Not only must the missionary have the right concept of his own ministry, but he must have faith in the power of the gospel to do for others what it has done for us. In the United States, in the early days with hearts aflame, even day laborers went out to preach the gospel. God honored them with ministries and gifts of the Spirit. Now can we have faith in God to do the same for others, regardless of the color of their skin? Or do we disbelieve in His power to work in this manner among other races and in other lands?

3

SELF-GOVERNMENT

The three basic elements which make the church indigenous are self-propagation, self-support and self-government. Where any one of these essential elements is missing, the church is not truly indigenous. We are now to consider *how* the missionary may proceed in order to assure the development of these necessary factors in the national church.

IMPORTANCE OF SELF-GOVERNMENT

It is usually granted that of these three aspects, self-government is the most difficult to accomplish and requires the longest time for achievement. Yet the principle of self-government is so important and the result in the spiritual life of the church so vital, that if we fail here, it could well mean that we shall fail in the entire program of establishing the indigenous church. Self-government makes for a sense of spiritual responsibility which will be reflected in self-support and self-propagation. To fail to place the responsibility of self-government on the converts is to choke their initiative and dwarf their spiritual growth. Furthermore, the rising tide of nationalism in every quarter of the earth demands that the national church be freed from the domination of foreign missionaries. The national converts will doubtless welcome the missionary's leadership in the beginning, but they will not be content for long if the management of the church remains in foreign hands.

If the missionary fails to recognize this legitimate desire for independence, and to work along with it, sooner or later dissatisfaction will result. Then an ultranationalistic agitator may appear and the frustration, buried deep in the hearts of the converts because they have not been given their proper place in the work, will come to the surface. As a result, the missionary will have the makings of a division on his hands. The dissatisfied group may even decide that it is necessary to split off in order to be able to govern their own affairs. Many such splits could have been avoided in the past if the proper steps to establish self-government had been taken in time.

> To assume that any native church perpetually requires constant supervision by a missionary is an unintended insult to their capacity to manage their own affairs. The most primitive tribes have some form of local and tribal government, adjusted to existing conditions. Necessity and common sense, even among the most backward and primitive, have so required. How much more then, may those same natives, now washed by the blood of Calvary's Lamb, enlightened by the Word of God, and filled with the Holy Ghost, give wise administration to the church and Community.[1]

SELF-GOVERNMENT BEGINS WITH LOCAL CHURCH

Perhaps we have made the mistake of thinking of self-government primarily on a national level rather than in terms of the local church. A national organization in the hands of inexperienced converts would, in the beginning, present almost insurmountable obstacles. But the government of local churches according to the New Testament pattern is not beyond the capacity of the national converts, even though they may be limited as to educational advantages. It is quite evident that there were hundreds of organized local assemblies in the early church before the apostles and elders came

[1]George R. Upton in *India Witness*, periodical of Methodist Publishing House, Lucknow, North India.

together in Jerusalem for the first "General Council."
In certain areas, it would appear that we have started
at the wrong level.

> It is unwise to organize a Church out of missionaries
> and their families before there are native Christians,
> and a presbytery or conference out of foreign mission-
> aries before there are native pastors. . . . Such a policy
> is apt to force the premature organization of ecclesias-
> tical machinery on the mission field. It creates a
> Church that will always be foreign in spirit. The
> natives come in one by one and find the foreigners in
> control, and they regard the whole institution as alien.[2]

We have set up an organization at the top level,
among missionaries, with perhaps a small number of
the most capable workers included, and have hoped that
in time organized self-government would filter down
to the local church level. In doing this we have started
at the wrong place. In order to have any real foundation in self-government, we must begin with the local
church. Granted that it may be a slower process, it is
nevertheless simpler, and the organizational structure
will be laid on a firmer foundation.

Local churches, properly functioning, are the fundamental units of the later, united fellowship. If the missionary is able to organize his converts into local
churches, then he has a powerful medium for evangelism and the essential basis for self-government. No
matter how many converts there are, or how many
workers, if we have not enabled them to form themselves into local, self-governing churches, then we do
not have an indigenous church. The first step in self-
government then, is the founding of properly organized
local churches throughout the district. Any national
organization that may exist later is for the purpose of
serving the local churches and aiding in the extension
of the work beyond the local sphere.

[2]A. J. Brown, *The Foreign Missionary*, p. 316.

NECESSITY OF RIGHT BEGINNING

Since with the establishment of the first local church we cast the mold for the pattern that subsequent churches are likely to follow, it is of utmost importance that we make a good beginning. Otherwise changes must be made later and changes are difficult. The foundation of self-government should be laid with the first church. If the missionary makes all the decisions at the beginning, the converts will become accustomed to his leadership. And later when they should take the responsibility for the management of their own affairs, he will find that they are unable, even unwilling, to do so.

> The temptation [to the missionary] . . . to carry on certain features of the government of the church is almost irresistible. Is the missionary not the father of the church? . . . Therefore, the various items related to the government of the church from the very start have been indicated by the wisdom of the missionary. It is difficult for the nationals to carry on the work independent of the missionary. They have from the start depended on his wisdom and they continue to do so as the church grows. It is only the energy of the Holy Spirit coupled with resistance within the soul of the missionary that will turn over all the factors involved in the government of the church—all its committees, its treasurership, trusteeship, its discipline, its preaching and teaching functions to the nationals. All of it must be by the local members.[3]

Now for a few suggestions as to practical steps that may be taken to establish a local church on a self-governing basis. Having won a group of converts, the missionary turns from being an evangelist to the function of teacher and instructs them in the precepts of the Christian faith and the standards of Christian living. The Great Commission emphasizes the teaching aspect of the missionary's ministry: "Go ye therefore and teach all nations."

[3]"A Study of Indigenous Policies and Procedures," p. 3, paper of the Conservative Baptist Foreign Mission Society.

The object of the teaching is to enable the converts to arrive at a clear understanding of Christian faith and conduct.

AGREEMENT ON FUNDAMENTALS

I think it can be readily seen that there must be a standard of doctrine and conduct accepted in common by the believers or else a true Christian church will not emerge. Every established congregation has some kind of standard, written or unwritten, even including those groups that do not profess to believe in a creed or organization. Their standard may be unwritten, but they have a common understanding and agreement as to points they consider vital.

To say that the Bible alone is the basis of fellowship is scarcely sufficient, for there is no region, remote though it be, whose isolation provides security from the presence of false teachers. Groups such as the Seventh-Day Adventists and Jehovah's Witnesses say that they too are guided by the Bible. Agreement on certain basic points is fundamental to fellowship (cf. I Cor. 1:10). For example, there is common agreement that a person must be born of God's Spirit before he may become a member of a church. He must also "bring forth fruits" that indicate a true repentance and a genuine experience with God.

Independent groups of believers without church government or discipline usually mean that everyone does that which is right in his own eyes. Under such circumstances unhealthy and unscriptural practices may develop.

When a missionary has gathered together a group of converts with the purpose of forming a church, he should first discuss with them their particular problems with the object of enabling them to reach common agreement as to biblical doctrine and standards of conduct. For example, in a country where common-law marriage is practiced, they doubtless will decide that the active membership should be limited to those who are legally married. About this and similar problems they must reach an understanding. These agreements may be published in a pamphlet with appropriate Scripture references and become the guide for the establishing of local congregations, the exercising of church discipline, etc. This can never result if the brethren fail to reach a basis of agreement.

It is vital that the converts themselves reach an understanding of the Christian life based on the Scriptures, so that their faith is firmly grounded and they are able to "give an answer to every man that asketh . . . a reason of the hope . . ." (I Peter 3:15). Then they will be prepared to begin to work together intelligently as a church. It is not absolutely necessary that such an agreement be published in pamphlet form (though the convenience of such a method can readily be visualized); a list of Scripture references under appropriate headings, left on record in the church, may suffice.

One point deserves special emphasis. The standard of doctrine and conduct must be an expression of the converts' own concept of the Christian life as they find it in the Scriptures. It is not enough that it be the missionary's belief. This is a vital distinction. Nothing is to be gained by taking our ideas and forcing them on the converts, as much as to say, "Here is our set of rules. If you are to be a member of our church, this is what you must do."

Instead, we must come together and patiently sit with them, a day or a year, as the occasion requires, until we have reached an understanding. It is to be *their* church, so it must be *their* standard. They are to carry on after we are gone. If it is the missionary's standard and not their own, they will do nothing about it when the missionary is not there to see that it is enforced. But if the truth of the Scriptures has gripped the mind of the convert, then he will feel, "I must do this, not because the missionary says so, but because it is the teaching of God's Word."

CHARTER MEMBERS

Once agreement is reached as to the standard of membership in the proposed church, there follows a second step, the choosing of the charter members. The missionary will request those who desire to become members of the kind of church that they have studied about, to make it known. Then, with the consent of the group, he may choose out three or four of the most dependable and mature converts, requesting them to serve with him as an examining committee.

This committee will review the list of candidates for membership one by one. The candidates will be examined as to their Christian experience, testimony and faithfulness. The question should be asked the committee members "So-and-so desires to be a member. Should he be accepted?" As the names are mentioned, the missionary should endeavor to arrive at the true opinion of the nationals. This requires patience and tact because people of other lands usually are not noted for their frankness. Sometimes there will be a ready answer, "Oh yes, this man is very sincere and faithful." Again, they may be reluctant to express themselves. The missionary may tactfully do a bit of probing since there may be something in the life of the individual of which the missionary is not aware. He may find it wise to leave the committee alone to discuss the matter among themselves for a moment. Perhaps the decision will be that the candidate should wait a little longer and give further proof of his sincerity.

In all this the missionary will be counseling and guiding, but not compelling. He will show them the importance of a good beginning; of keeping the work unsoiled, advising them not to be overanxious for large numbers, or to try to woo the rich and influential. Since the missionary is laying the foundation, he must proceed with care.

If the committee is in doubt, the missionary should

endeavor to guide them by referring to the Holy Scripture. That is an authority that they will honor, and one to which they themselves can appeal. Thus they will see that the authority rests in the Word of God and not with the missionary.

When the list is complete, one of the members of the committee will be appointed to read it to the whole group of converts. If a candidate has not been approved for membership, then in order to avoid offending sensitive natures, it should be pointed out that this is not a denial of membership, but merely a delay in order to give time for further instruction and Christian growth.

The group of converts should be given opportunity to express their approval of the work of the committee and to ask any question concerning the decisions. When this is done in the right way, the converts feel that this is truly their church and their responsibility. Therefore, it is profitable for the missionary to follow this method, even though he may be perfectly sure that every candidate will be accepted. He is doing more than accepting candidates; he is training the church in self-government.

BAPTIZING CONVERTS

The next step will be to give Christian baptism to those who have been approved. The question has been asked, Should the missionary baptize the national converts? Obviously he will have to do so at first. St. Paul baptized when occasion required, but he did not consider it an essential part of his missionary ministry (I Cor. 1:14-17). The missionary will be wise to follow the apostle's example in this and insist that as soon as there are recognized national workers, they perform this sacred rite. In the writer's opinion, all recognized pastors should be allowed to baptize their converts and administer the Lord's Supper (in cooperation with the official board). Thus the church will not be deprived of the sacraments so necessary to its growth and spiritual life. Certainly a missionary should not reserve for himself the exclusive right to perform these sacraments after there are recognized national workers. To do so can only weaken the indigenous church and belittle the workers in the eyes of their countrymen.

Following baptism, the names of the candidates should be listed as the charter members of the church. As new members are added from time to time, they should be examined by the church board, with perhaps the guidance of the missionary, at least for the first few times. Our Central American churches hold regular weekly classes for new converts previous to baptism, and ordinarily a continual stream of converts is passing through them. It may require two to three months for them to complete the studies. In the meantime, the majority of the adults must take the necessary steps to meet the requirements of civil marriage. During this period they are introduced into the life and activities of the church. When the day comes for their public baptism, it is indeed a high point in their lives.

Our Central American pastors will not baptize anyone who does not meet the requirements for church membership. "Why," they ask, "should we baptize a man who has no intentions of meeting our standards? We do not want him announcing to outsiders that we have baptized him, if he is not producing the fruit of a convert." Hence all baptized converts are immediately received as members of the church. I do not insist on this point for other fields, but personally I agree with our pastors.

To a casual observer this method of introducing converts into the life of the church and the privileges of membership may seem unnecessarily slow. The object, however, is for them to understand their privileges and responsibilities in becoming part of the church. They must be made to realize the fact that it is *their* church. What a difference this makes!

CHOOSING OFFICIALS

Now that the church has come into existence, the next step is to provide it with the necessary officials.

The pastor may be chosen first. The missionary will doubtless find it necessary to guide the proceedings by suggestions and counsel, but the decision must rest with the congregation. If a certain worker has been God's instrument in bringing the assembly into being, the choice of the brethren may fall upon him. Or it may be that among the converts themselves there is a man of recognized spiritual leadership—a man whom the others naturally look to and follow. The church may desire him as its pastor. In such a case, he may be regarded as "temporary" pastor to care for the church until a more mature man is available, or until he himself develops in his ministry to the point where he may be recognized as the regular pastor.

The election of deacons will follow next. It will be necessary for the missionary to remind the church of the scriptural qualifications required to fill the office of a deacon. The group may wish to name a nominating committee which, under the guidance of the missionary, will then present to the church the names of those eligible to fill the office, so that the church can make its selection from among them.

PROVIDING LEADERSHIP FOR NEW GROUPS

In several of the Central American republics, the churches have a rather useful custom. They elect first, second and third deacons.[4] Then when the church is without a regular pastor, or when the pastor is temporarily absent, the first deacon is in charge. When he

[4]This use of the office of deacon doubtless approximates the ministry of the New Testament *elders* rather than that of deacons; and to be completely scriptural, probably they should be so designated. However, the principle involved in the practice of deacons developing a spiritual ministry beyond the "serving of tables" has the approbation of New Testament precedent in the cases of Stephen and Philip (Acts 6-8).

is absent, the second deacon takes over. In this way
there is no question as to who should bear the responsibility of leadership. The deacons are chosen with this
thought in mind so that the more capable men are
placed in these positions. On the whole the practice
has proved very satisfactory, with many such deacons
having developed their ministry to such an extent that
they have become full-time workers.

The question may well be asked: Where in a new
work do you find men to fill adequately the office of
deacon? Naturally this is not always possible. Some
sort of government, however, is necessary, even in the
newest church,[5] so we may fill the gap with a temporary board. In this case, we make use of the best material available, but we do not call these men deacons,
but *encargados,* which in Spanish means "the ones in
charge." This temporary board serves until brethren
of spiritual maturity develop in the church. Then a
regular board should be elected. Such temporary measures are often necessary when a revival sweeps a section and groups of believers spring up with no experienced workers available. We cannot allow these groups
to drift along without leadership. Many such groups
have developed splendidly under the leadership of
these temporary boards.

The Apostle Paul committed his converts to the care
and guidance of the Holy Spirit and to the grace of
God. He did not think that it was necessary to continue with them for long periods of time in order to

[5]We believe that we are not far from the apostolic pattern in
providing leadership from among the converts early in the life of
the local church. "According to Ramsay, St. Paul preached in
Lystra for about six months on his first missionary journey, then
he ordained elders and left for about eighteen months. After that
he visited the Church for the second time, but only spent a few
months in the province. Then for the last time, after an interval
of three years, he visited them again, but again he was only a
month or two in the province. From this it is clear that the
Churches of Galatia were really founded and established in the
first visit" (Roland Allen, *Missionary Methods: St. Paul's or
Ours?,* p. 111).

keep them from failure. If we exercise faith in God, He will help both them and us.

If the congregation in question springs up in the same locality where the missionary resides and there is no local pastor, the missionary must exercise special care. He must not continue year after year to make all the decisions for the congregation or do all the preaching. The danger that antagonism may result has already been pointed out.

A second danger should be mentioned: that of spoiling the people so that at a later date they will not be satisfied to accept anyone less than a missionary as their pastor. Compared with the preaching ministry and efficient administration of the missionary, the abilities of an inexperienced national worker are likely to appear quite deficient. To prevent the development of such a situation, the missionary will do well to choose, early in the life of the new church, a deacon or brother who shows promise of usefulness and, with the consent of the congregation, give him at least partial responsibility for the work. The missionary may be able to overcome any reluctance on the part of the believers to accept this arrangement by explaining to them his own responsibility to the other towns and villages of the district. He must point out that he will fail in his mission if he is required to give all of his time to the care of one church. When the matter is presented in this light, the converts will more readily accept the appointed brother as their pastor, or at least, as copastor with the missionary.

WITHDRAWAL OF MISSIONARY FROM LOCAL CHURCH

Under this arrangement, it may be necessary for the missionary to continue his guidance for a time. He will help occasionally with the preaching, but he should plan to withdraw more and more from the local affairs until he can leave them entirely in the hands of the nationals. Frequent, extended trips into the district will help him to withdraw, and the converts will become accustomed to the leadership of the national pastor. Here is where the missionary should sincerely try "to work himself out of a job." For he is building a church, and a church must have its own national pastor to be complete.

As a congregation assumes the responsibility of self-government, it is important that the national pastor be shown the steps he should take in order to maintain good relations with the official board and congregation, and to promote the efficient administration of the church.

An important step will be the holding of regular business sessions. In the beginning, sessions should be held at least once a month, one with the official board first, and one with the membership. The pastor should receive instructions as to procedure in presiding over the sessions, both as to elementary parliamentary law, and as to his personal attitude. Thus he may avoid the pitfalls of profitless discussions and angry tempers.

BUSINESS SESSIONS

The private session with the official board may be held the week before the general session with the congregation. A secretary should be instructed to keep a record of the proceedings in both sessions, and these minutes should be kept with the church records. The pastor will preside at the session of the official board unless otherwise agreed upon. After prayer, he will read a list of the matters to be discussed and then ask the members of the board if they have any point for discussion that they would like to add to the list. When the agenda is complete, he will present the first point for discussion and, when a decision is reached, pass on to the next point.

Generally the points to be discussed will include some of the following: Approval of candidates for baptism, cases of discipline when sins have been committed by members of the congregation, counsel and exhortation to brethren requesting advice or needing spiritual help, difficulties that have arisen in the congregation, advance moves planned to benefit the local church. Even though the pastor may not be aware of any special problem, he should call the church board for a session at the regularly appointed time. Often problems exist of which he may not be aware. Should there be no problems, it will still be of great profit to the whole church and enrich the harmony among the leaders, if the time is spent in prayer and intercession for the spiritual progress of the church.

In the general session, the secretary will read the minutes of the previous session, give the financial report and read the decisions of the official board reached in the private session. Candidates approved for baptism and members to receive discipline should be publicly announced. Approval of the action of the board in these cases should be given by voting. Any member should have liberty to ask questions or suggest matters for discussion by the church. The church, by voting, can disapprove of the decisions of the church board, or request reconsideration of a question.

A missionary, when present in a session—and especially if called upon to preside—should encourage correct procedure, but should not be overinsistent on the niceties of parliamentary law. He must be prepared for a considerable amount of informal discussion. He should encourage full and free discussion of all doubtful points in order to arrive at a satisfactory solution. Above all, let his teaching and example emphasize the fact that differences of opinion need not cause a rift in spiritual unity, and that Christians can learn to express their opinions without indulging in carnal and personal feelings.

RESPONSIBILITY FOR DISCIPLINE

An essential aspect of self-government is the disciplining of members. This is often a difficult and unpleasant task. *Let the missionary beware of acting alone in questions of discipline.* This is a responsibility that should be shared by the entire church. A missionary zealous for the good name of the church may feel that the question of discipline is too difficult for inexperienced Christians, and decide to act for the church. In following this course, he may attempt to investigate the case; if he finds that the report is true, he may prematurely instruct the secretary to strike the offender's name from the membership list, or restrict his privileges for a certain period.

What is the result of such procedure? Discipline so administered is usually ineffective. The offender has influence; his relatives and friends are members of the church and often they will openly sympathize with him. Officials who carry out the order escape personal responsibility for the act by saying that they are merely carrying out the missionary's instructions. Hence, the church does not back up the missionary in his action. The reputation of the church is not cleared nor the offender truly disciplined, for he has not smarted under the disapproval of his fellow Christians. Instead of the church dealing out discipline as a body, the whole affair appears to have degenerated into a personal difference between the offender and the missionary. Consequently, the church lags in spiritual development and becomes less competent to handle such cases. Moreover, the good that the missionary hoped to achieve by taking the matter in his own hands has not resulted, since the church has not been purged by true repentance from the leaven of sin that contaminated it.

Yet, examples are easily found where churches, left to their own devices, have lapsed into moral indifference and have failed to exercise necessary restraint upon sinning members. What is to be done in such a case? Roland Allen in *Missionary Methods: St. Paul's or Ours?* presents the case well:

> Nevertheless, when individuals broke through all bounds and committed flagrant offences he [St. Paul] did not hesitate to insist upon the need of discipline. There is a point at which the conscience of the whole

Church ought to be stirred to protest, when for the Church to pass over an offence in silence is to deny her claim to be a moral society. It is in just such cases that the Church is often slow to act. Comparatively small offences are sometimes visited with stern severity: horrible crimes shock the whole congregation, but none dares to move.

Such an offence was committed at Corinth. . . . St. Paul could not avoid moving in the matter, but he obviously did so with great reluctance. It is quite clear that he was determined in the last resort to take action himself, but it is equally clear that he was most anxious to avoid it. He wished the Church to realize its responsibility, and to act as a body. . . . He wrote to accuse the Church of its failure to realize its duty in the matter. In a case of this kind, according to his view, the Church, as a Church, had a duty to perform, a duty to the offender and a duty to itself. To shirk that duty was criminal. Therefore he waited to see if the Church would do its duty before he interfered himself. In the result the Church did respond to his exhortation, the offender was excommunicated by the majority, he accepted his discipline, he repented, he was restored. . . .

We look upon the sting of excommunication as exclusion from spiritual privileges; but the man who so acts as to incur excommunication is often the last person to feel that sting. His spiritual apprehension has already been deadened before he falls into sin. What he needs is the public censure of the majority of his fellow-churchmen to awaken his conscience. If the majority of his fellow-churchmen do not avoid him and cast him out, it is little use for a formal sentence of exclusion from Church privileges to be issued against him and carried out by officials of the [mission] society alone. That does no good; it very often only does harm. It hardens the man without humbling or instructing him.

Moreover, an act of this kind is done not only for the good of the offender, but for the good of the Church. It is meant to clear the Church's good name which has been sullied by the act of one of its members. . . . But if the majority feel that they have not a real share in the action of the Church, if they do not heartily and sincerely realize that the act is their own act, if they consequently do not support it, then there is no real clearance of the Church. Nominally the man is excommunicated . . . but if, in fact, this has only been the act of a few officials, then in reality there is no clearance. Christians and heathen alike recognize that the leaders of the Church have expressed their disapproval. Christians and heathen alike recognize that the body has done nothing of the kind.

In this case at Corinth we see St. Paul's principle of mutual responsibility again enforced, and he enforced it by staying away from Corinth until the Church had realized and executed its duty. . . . St. Paul stirred and educated the conscience of the whole Corinthian Church. If he had sent a letter of excommunication to the . . . Church, none of those effects would have followed. . . . He threw upon them the responsibility and trusted to them to learn in what way it was to be fulfilled. In the last resort he threatened to intervene, if they refused to do their duty, but it was only after he had exercised all his powers to make intervention unnecessary.

Therefore he succeeded through failure where we often fail through succeeding. We exercise discipline and leave the Church undisciplined. He disciplined the Church; we discipline individuals. He left the Church, and it stood, tottering on its feet, but still standing; we leave the Church without any power of standing at all.[6]

We have seen very satisfactory results from placing the problems and responsibility of discipline directly upon the church. Rather than this resulting in moral laxity in the church, we have often found that the nationals are inclined to be more rigid in their disciplinary action than we ourselves would have been; so much so, that when we have been called upon for counsel, we have more often found it necessary to stress the need for the spirit of grace in dealing with the offender

[6]*Ibid.*, pp. 159-63.

rather than to exhort them not to pass lightly over an offense.

Again, the nationals know their own people and have a way of arriving at the facts of a case that would be almost impossible for a foreigner. Thus by making the church itself responsible for the disciplining of its members, the missionary avoids many a costly mistake, and at the same time increases the sense of responsibility among the members.

We have found it satisfactory for the official board of the church to serve as an investigating committee, giving the church its recommendation on action to be taken. Thus the church as a body acts in the case, pronouncing the disciplinary action without the necessity of scandalous details being made known to immature members.

An unwise custom is followed by some churches who secretly take the name of an offending member off the church roll. This not only lays the pastor or officials open to charges of having been motivated by personal prejudice, but it also is completely ineffective in bringing about repentance in the individual concerned, and in clearing the good name of the church. Discipline to be effective must be applied by the majority of the church body. Our experience has been that when it is thus applied, it indeed preserves the norm of the church and often restores the offender.

4

SELF-PROPAGATION

Self-propagation is the vital element of the missionary program and the true objective of the missionary endeavor, because a church which does not propagate itself will soon die out. New Testament churches were self-propagating.

Indigenous church principles recognize the local church unit as the best medium for evangelism. When we have established a local church with all of its rightful and inherent vigor, we have followed God's own method for propagating the gospel.

Every Convert a Witness

Converts are seed—gospel seed. The field is the world and the seed are the children of the kingdom (Matt. 13:38). Each convert is seed for a potential harvest. By nature, new converts are enthusiastic witnesses because their vital experience with Christ has made them zealous to impart their new-found knowledge to others. Missionaries must learn to utilize that God-given zeal. It has been said that the Korean Church requires each new convert to win someone to Christ before he himself can qualify for baptism. It is vital that each convert be a soul-winner.

Putting Converts to Work

Happy is the missionary who has the gift of putting his converts to work. He will see results for his labors far out of proportion to those which follow the labors of a hard-working missionary without this ability.

In this regard many missionaries fail. They insist on

personally supervising every move and are unwilling to turn the converts loose. These missionaries are always overworked with the visiting of outstations and the conducting of services. While I admire their zeal and energy, yet I feel that they work a hardship on themselves and do an injustice to the work. It has been said that it is better to put ten men to work than to do the work of ten men. When the missionary puts the church to work, he not only gets more accomplished, but the church develops in the process. Activity and responsibility make for growth.

We should be careful not to discourage the enthusiasm of a new convert for witnessing by being over-anxious to get everything "under control." Most missionaries have known of new converts who in their zeal have gone out, perhaps to their own village, and won several others by their testimony, sometimes even before they themselves have been baptized. The missionary will make a mistake if he sets this zealous convert to one side in order to send a trained worker in his stead. A common result is that the work done by the new convert withers and dies; for the mission-trained worker is not able to carry on. The zeal of the convert who has been set aside is likely to subside, for he gets the impression that he is not really capable of being an effective witness. Or else why did the missionary send someone else in his place? Thus a promising worker is discouraged. The proper step is to encourage and teach the convert so that he can develop along the right lines. Roland Allen states: "We ought never to send a Mission agent to do what men are already doing on the spot spontaneously."

In Central America, the churches open what they term *campos blancos,* literally, "whitened fields." These are outstations, not of the mission station, but of the church. The churches have an average of two or three outstations each, and some have as many as twelve. Each church is considered responsible for the evangelization of the surrounding territory, at least halfway to the next church. These outstations have been opened in a simple manner. Perhaps one of the members who lived a considerable distance from the church opened his home for the preaching of the gospel. Or some unconverted person who, for reasons of family ties or previous knowledge of the gospel, was sympathetically disposed, may have desired meetings in his house.

EVANGELISM BY EXTENSION OF THE LOCAL CHURCH

Instead of making these outstations the care of the missionary, the churches appoint their best qualified men to supervise them. They assign a certain lay worker to a given preaching point, making him responsible for that station for a period of time—perhaps for six months. They give him a letter signed by the church officials so that he may avoid trouble with the local authorities. If he is faithful in his task, the church will doubtless permit him to continue this activitiy. Christians consider it an honor to be chosen for such ministry and are glad for an opportunity to work for the Lord. Often they go out two by two, perhaps walking a long distance once or twice a week to care for their outstation. There is no thought of financial remuneration—it is their service to the Lord.

LAY PREACHERS

Occasionally the lay worker will be given opportunity to report the progress of his outstation to the main church. Sometimes the congregation sends a small group to accompany each local worker to his respective outstation to contribute with song and testimony to the success of the service. Sometimes a revival breaks out in the outstation and the main church will feel the throb of new life as the new converts come in to fill the ranks. Thus the whole assembly shares in the spreading of the gospel. The pastor visits these stations as he is able, but often the local workers carry on without help for weeks at a time.

The organization of the Sunday school for evangelism is a very practical way for developing new workers and for opening new outstations, with the pastor using the Sunday school as a basis for outreach. The pastor first trains the teachers in special classes to teach the Sunday school lesson; sometimes they are provided with flannelboard and figures to make the lesson more easily taught, and more interesting. Then a survey is made in the entire area surrounding the church to see where the branch Sunday schools could be opened. Members of the church offer their homes; friends may be requested to give space in their living room or in their patio; and sometimes the only location available is under a tree or in a park. The pastor then assigns the teachers to the different areas. The results have been truly amazing. One pastor has a membership of approximately eighty people with a working Sunday school staff of about twenty-five workers. They have reached as many as two thousand people in a single weekend in as many as seventy-five different branch Sunday school locations. The teachers do not simply teach the lesson once; as well as teaching in the regular class in the church, they teach as many as four or five times in different locations. Some begin their teaching as early as Saturday afternoon and continue through Sunday afternoon. It is only a step to convert such a branch Sunday school into a permanent outstation with regular preaching taking place.

Then in due time, if the work prospers, groups of converts form in these outstations. They receive instruction in Christian doctrine and conduct, in preparation for baptism, and presently another group is ready to be organized into a church. The pastor of the main church then talks the matter over with them, consulting with the presbyter of the district also. If it is agreed that the time is ripe for organizing the church, the group quite likely will ask the lay worker who has been instrumental in raising up the work to come to them as their pastor. They agree to bring him food and to pay their tithes.

A New Church Is Born

Perhaps this lay worker has in the meantime felt the hand of God upon his life leading him into a fuller ministry, and so is prepared to accept the call. Thus it often works out that we have not only a new church, but also a new worker. He in turn will begin to send out his converts into the surrounding territory, and the process begins all over again with the message of life reaching an ever widening area.

When the time comes for a short-term Bible school to open, there is no necessity of urging these young workers to attend. They have preached all they know, sometimes using the same message again and again, and are anxious to learn more. Furthermore, problems have arisen which they have been unable to solve. So when Bible school opens, they will be there.

If his church is not too far away, the worker will likely continue caring for it on weekends, returning to the school each Monday to continue his studies. If it is far, the deacons will have to carry on for him, with the help of neighboring pastors, during the four-month term. As for the new worker, we can be sure that he will not be an indifferent student. It is a real joy to minister to such men, giving to them the much needed teaching they so earnestly desire.

As a result of such activities in one section of El Salvador, there is an established church every eight or ten miles in almost every direction. Within a radius of some thirty miles there are at least one hundred self-supporting churches, each with its own pastor. Since each of these assemblies has from three to twelve lay preachers who are caring for outstations with new groups of believers constantly being formed, the work continues to expand.

One church, called Filadelfia, is located about eight miles from Santa Ana. It has a membership of less than one hundred. It would be larger but time after time it has given up a portion of its members to form the nucleus of a new church. This church has used about ten lay workers continually during the past years. These men carry the gospel week by week into the surrounding area and, as they develop their ministry, many of them become full-time workers.

This remarkable work is the product of the labors of a staunch national convert who had little talent as a preacher, but he had a clear vision of the work of the church and of the necessity of teaching his converts. He also had a remarkable capacity for pushing his converts into active service. He so established this church, and taught the converts, that they themselves now know how to establish a group of converts and form them into a local church without the aid of a missionary or national official. Some of the outstanding pastors and officials in El Salvador are a product of this church. The pastor who founded the church went to be with Christ a few years ago, but the church has maintained its vigorous program under successive pastors. At last count thirty-six pastors were serving in the work that had come from this one church. This group demonstrates the possibilities of self-propagation.

PIONEERING A NEW AREA

Now that we have observed the important role which the local churches play in the evangelization of a district where there is already a small beginning, let us examine the process by which a missionary may bring such a group of self-propagating churches into existence in a new district.

In pioneering a new area, the missionary exercises his first and most important ministry as a planter of churches. Here the missionary must be evangelist to the unconverted and teacher to the new-born converts. Instead of settling down to pastor the first group of converts that he raises up, the missionary should remain mobile and keep the vision for the entire district. He should become a sort of circuit rider, visiting the towns and villages in the district when favorable circumstances give him an opening. At all times he should give particular attention to those points where the Spirit of God seems to be moving in a special way, but refuse to stay in one place so long that the people come to depend upon him as their pastor.

TAKE PROMISING CONVERTS ALONG

When the missionary makes his monthly or bimonthly tour of the field, he will do well to encourage national brethren, who give promise of usefulness for God, to accompany him. Should he already have the help of a national worker with some experience in gospel work who perhaps has come from a neighboring district, so much the better. But, if not, let the missionary keep on the lookout for promising "Timothys" among the converts, inviting such to accompany him on his tours. Care should be taken from the first, however, that the missionary does not foster in the young worker a spirit of financial dependence upon himself by offering him financial remuneration or by assuming an undue portion of the travel expenses. The tour should be a partnership in the work of the gospel.

This companionship on the missionary trail has a fourfold purpose. First, it enables the missionary to inspire and instruct the young workers more effectively than he would be able to do in a classroom. Second, the need of the field and the opportunities for gospel work in the district, viewed with the missionary, are impressed upon the young worker, thus inspiring his evangelistic fervor and preparing him to answer God's call to meet the need which he has seen. Third, the new groups of believers become accustomed to the ministry of a national, rather than that of the missionary, so that when the moment comes for them to establish themselves as a local congregation, they will doubtless ask some such worker to come to them as their pastor. Last, the presence of nationals with the missionary inspires confidence in the hearers.

This intimate association helps the missionary to interpret correctly the attitudes, customs and problems which he finds. Thus he himself is educated in native ways and avoids what otherwise might be serious blunders in dealing with the people.

As groups of converts come into existence, the missionary will assume his second role, that of teacher. He will give instruction in Christian doctrine and conduct, then he will encourage them in the task of propagating the gospel, showing them how to go about the establishing of churches and outstations. After organizing the groups in the manner explained in the preceding chapter, he will leave them in charge of their own national leaders, with only an occasional visit to guide and inspire them.

EVANGELIZING LARGE CITIES

Today the metropolitan areas of the world form an unprecedented challenge to the church for evangelism. In Latin America, as in other parts of the world, the population is rushing to the cities. In several countries of Latin America, the population of the capital city is from one-fifth to one-third of the entire population of the country. This is a challenge that the church cannot ignore.

Some have questioned whether indigenous church principles would really work in the large city. My answer would be that they must work or we are doomed to failure. City people have the same basic need as other people. In fact, in some cases, with the great rush to the city, there are many displaced persons seeking a new life who are especially responsive to the gospel message.

One method that will work in the city is the church expansion plan explained earlier in this chapter. If the church has the proper vitality and spiritual motivation, it can multiply itself through outstations, which in turn become churches, until the entire city is reached. Too often, however, when a city church reaches a comfortable size, so that there is sufficient financial income to support its pastor and carry on normal activities, the

church relaxes and begins more and more to confine
its activities to within the four walls of its building.
Instead of recognizing its responsibility to reach the
whole city, often the church itself does not move out in
aggressive evangelism; and if some other pastor or group
tries to do this, it is resented as being an intrusion in
the area of the first church. I have been in a city where
the people only two or three blocks away from the
church did not know there was an evangelical church
in the area! So, what is needed first is a vision, and
next, vital spiritual life on the part of the congregation
itself.

Another way that a city can be reached is through
the establishing of a strong central church, either by a
missionary or a national, with the express purpose of
not only building up a strong congregation, but of
reaching the entire city and surrounding area with the
gospel. The Swedish Assemblies of God missionaries in
Brazil have followed this method with notable success.
They have clung tenaciously to the central-church idea,
and all of the other churches in a city are, theoretically
at least, supposed to be related to the main church. In
more recent times, this has been modified and auton-
omous churches are permitted in each major section
of the city. In this time of strong nationalistic tendencies, I would question the wisdom of a foreign missionary establishing himself as pastor of such a church for
an indefinite period of time. Rather, it is necessary to
push the national ministry to the front.

Then, we should not overlook the possibilities of
reaching the city through large campaigns. This has
been done with notable success in several areas of Latin
America. In El Salvador an evangelist held a ten-week
open-air campaign which resulted in the establishing
of twelve churches where previously there was only one,
and the increase in attendance in Sunday school from
about one hundred to fifteen hundred at the end of the
year—reaching a peak of nine thousand in three or four
years. Today these churches have multiplied until

there are approximately forty organized churches in this one city. Similarly, in Guatemala City a campaign resulted in the establishing of ten churches. In Uruguay, evangelists have gone into provincial capitals and, after a campaign of two or three months, have left a congregation of five to six hundred people. The secret in these cases has been the duration of the campaign; the evangelist stays from three to six months until the converts are well established. In the cases referred to, not only was salvation presented, but prayer was offered for the sick, and as a result many were healed; this attracted the multitudes. It is very important in this type of meeting for teaching to be given to the new converts while the campaign is still going on. It is too late to wait until the evangelist has gone to attempt to gather together the fruits of the campaign. When this has happened, sometimes the greater portion of the harvest has been lost. However, when teaching is given with the idea of preparing the new converts for baptism and church membership, and establishing them in the Word of God, the converts can be consolidated into a vital church.

Regardless of the method used in reaching a city or community, an important factor is the active participation of members and converts.

Another system that has been used with success in smaller towns, is for the believers and pastors of a neighboring town or towns to make an all-out effort in a new city. Preparations are made beforehand; permits are requested for street meetings or for preaching in other public places; and groups of Christians converge on the town for three or four days, distributing literature from house to house, inviting people to the services and doing personal work. Then an evangelist—preferably a national—climaxes with a few days of evangelistic meetings. Such a united effort has resulted in the establishing of a new congregation in a town where previously it has been most difficult to get a foothold.

5

DEVELOPING LEADERSHIP

The government and extension of the church in any land must eventually be left in the hands of national leaders. These men are Christ's own gift to His church (Eph. 4:11-13). Without such men, the task of establishing an indigenous church would be hopeless. Since it is precisely at this point that many missions have failed, we shall endeavor to point out some of the mistakes of the past, giving also some constructive suggestions.

Let us again bring our objective into clear focus. Our aim is to develop the national church rather than the mission station. We are to provide leadership for the national church, not merely helpers for the missionary. Missionaries often unconsciously reflect a wrong concept when they talk about "my helper" or "my worker." The national pastor or evangelist is Christ's gift to His church, not to the missionary. Let us begin by asking some questions:

What Do We Want? Our objectives should include the following:

First, our workers training program should aim at developing spiritual, soul-winning churches.

Second, the immediate objective should be the preparation of lay workers and full-time workers to man an expanding program of evangelism and care for the new churches that thus will be raised up.

Third, the long-range program calls for the preparation of spiritual leaders in all spheres of ministry so that they will be able to carry on a fully developed, indigenous church program.

Are We Reaching Our Objectives?

While we rejoice in the evidence of very good results which we have seen, and praise God for the consecrated effort of every missionary, as well as the dedication of the national workers, there is probably not one among us who is completely satisfied. The most optimistic among us would admit that we are only partially reaching these objectives. Here are some of the less flattering facts which we must face:

First, many of the churches raised up are not truly soul-winning agencies of the kingdom of God. Those that are reasonably active and successful are usually not functioning to the maximum of their potential, while others are almost entirely unproductive in this respect.

Second, many of the pastors and workers produced by mission schools have not turned out to be real soul-winners nor have manifested true spiritual leadership. While there are notable exceptions, many times workers lack initiative and depend too much on the mission for guidance and financial support. This is not intended to be an indictment of either the missionary or the worker.

Something has been missing, and neither the missionary nor the worker may know what it is! It is not necessarily lack of consecration, nor lack of love to God, although few of us would claim that our spiritual life could not be improved in this regard!

Third, some workers seem to feel that after they have been to school they are above pioneering a church or working in rural areas. Perhaps this is a reflection of the general modern movement toward the large cities. However, we cannot doubt that there is a measure of failure in our training program if the men we are training are unwilling to return to the churches and the

areas with which they are familiar and which present
a great spiritual challenge. In this case, we are at least
partially training them *away* from the task instead of
for the task.

Where Have We Failed? It may be that there are gaps
in our training program.

First, there may be a gap between the intellectual
development and the spiritual development of the
worker. Too often we have trained the mind and have
not been able to lead the student into the full life in
the Holy Spirit.

Second, there may be a gap between knowledge and
practical ministry. We place a student in school and
nurture him in a somewhat artificial climate. He is
often too far removed for too long a period of time from
the rugged life and problems which he is to meet in the
ministry.

Third, we may have left too wide a gap between the
clergy and the laity. Our training program should aim
to put the entire church on the march for God.

Fourth, there may be a serious gap in our concept of
the role that the training of workers plays in the development of the church. Some train only to fill va-
cancies. A Latin American minister in a kindly way
voiced his criticism of our workers' training program,
saying that we were training too many prospective
workers. He said his own denomination looked ahead
and saw that in the future they would need six or seven
more pastors. Then they trained that number and,
when a class finished seminary work, there was a place
assured for each one. There was no question of support
nor what this worker would do. On the other hand, he
said, "You train more workers than you have openings
for, and then many must fill an inferior place or get
along without support." My answer to that is that we
are training workers for invasion. We do not expect
merely to hold our own, but we expect to train far more

workers than we have churches. We believe that this is the way that new churches will come into existence. A man trained under the other concept would not be expected to exercise personal initiative. Someone else would do the planning for him and finance his efforts. I fear that following such a concept would never permit us to evangelize the world in our generation.

Fifth, we may be neglecting to train the right men. It is important that the missionary shall not limit his leadership training to the bright young men who at first glance would appear to be the best material. This is one of the fundamental errors of modern missions. The missionary has failed to see the importance of making place for mature men—the "elders" of the New Testament. Instead, he has gathered around him a group of the brightest minds, usually boys from the mission school or children of converts, to give them special instruction. One missionary stated his policy in these words: "He [the missionary] lays hold of the best elements of the race [i.e., young boys of quick intelligence] to whom he ministers, training them into a force which he can use."

These boys are kept on the mission station at mission expense over a period of years. If they prove to be apt students, they become assistants to the foreign missionary, at times performing tasks at the station, at other times taking short evangelistic trips into the surrounding territory to distribute literature or to hold gospel services. They may be given charge at outstations. Later they may be sent to a theological seminary, and afterward placed in charge of churches under the oversight of the missionary.

But often, just when the missionary begins to hope that he is accomplishing his task of providing a trained, national ministry for the church, he finds that deepseated troubles exist; that in spite of all of their training, his national workers are inadequate. This inadequacy is sometimes intangible and difficult to analyze. One or more weaknesses may be present.

COMMON INADEQUACIES OF MISSION-TRAINED WORKERS

For one thing, the worker may not be able to *lead* the national church. Perhaps he preaches well but his fellow countrymen do not really accept him as their leader. They constantly appeal to the missionary over the head of the local pastor, or else they follow the advice of strong lay leaders in the congregation whose ideas are often opposed to those of the pastor.

Then, he may lack initiative. He waits for the missionary to tell him to visit a new locality. Even when he goes, he often is not able to make the most of the opportunities presented.

Again, he may experience difficulty in adjusting himself to the humble surroundings of the community to which he ministers, feeling that to adapt himself to the lowly customs of the villagers would be a step down for him.

Also, he may continue to depend on the missionary to meet his financial needs and be unable to demonstrate a robust faith in God.

In such circumstances, a missionary may become discouraged with the worker and decide that it was a mistake to have trained him. He may even despair of ever being able to train national converts for successful leadership. Before he reaches such an unhappy conclusion, the missionary would do well to reflect that such national workers are not entirely to blame for their inadequacy. Let us observe the causes that have produced these deficiencies.

CAUSES OF INADEQUACIES

The worker's training from boyhood has largely been under semiforeign influence and under circumstances which have separated him from his national environment.

Furthermore, he has been trained in Western learning rather than in the wisdom of his race. Consequently, he seems to his own people to be half foreign. They do not easily accept him as their leader because his ways are different, and in some cases, even his style of speech has been affected.

It is true that he lacks initiative. Has he not all his life been subject to the rule of the missionary? He has always been corrected and sometimes punished when he failed to do as the missionary desired. If he displeases the missionary now, the missionary has power to remove him from his position and church. His only safety lies in obeying the missionary and in making sure that he doesn't displease him. Is it any wonder that he lacks initiative?

Granted that he looks too much to the missionary for his support. What else could be expected? Has not the missionary always provided for him, first in school, then in his outstation work, afterward in the seminary and finally in his pastorate? The training of his whole life has been one of dependence upon the missionary. It is too much to expect that a lifetime of training can be overcome just because he has now become a pastor of a church. This is especially true when the missionary still handles the funds and allots the salaries.

What Must We Do?

We must seek the New Testament approach and follow the New Testament pattern. I have the deep conviction that every deficiency in our work can be traced to a failure to follow the New Testament pattern. True indigenous church principles are in reality New Testament church principles. We might be shocked if we could bring ourselves face to face with the discrepancies between our methods and the New Testament pattern. We may be completely orthodox in our *theology* and be a long way from the New Testament example in our *practice*. How easy it is to accept the established pattern as the right pattern! We think it is right because our predecessors followed this way or it is the pattern established by other missions. Yet experience is teaching us that the established modern pattern of missions is not sufficient to meet the demands of the day. We will never reach the world for Christ in our generation if we simply follow in the groove worn for us by our predecessors. The New Testament approach is a *flexible* approach. It leaves room for the guidance of the Holy Spirit. Not all situations are to be met in the same way. This brings up a very serious question. Are we spiritual leaders of a sufficient stature to be able to determine the mind of God for the problems of our particular field, or will we insist on following through on a predetermined course? I would like to break this down into a few practical suggestions.

First, we must provide for the spiritual development of our prospective workers as well as their intellectual development. Jesus chose the disciples first of all that they might "be with Him" and after that they should preach and heal the sick. Many times He called His disciples apart for spiritual instruction. He took them with Him in the ministry and, as far as they were able to follow, through Gethsemane and Calvary. In a very real sense, they went with Him through the resurrection. Even so, He required that they spend ten days waiting in Jerusalem for the fullness of the Spirit before they were to go "into all the world." Too often in modern practice we have neglected this phase of training. We train in theology, homiletics and church history, but how seldom do our students learn the deeper meanings of the cross, the resurrection and the indwelling Spirit!

Second, we must integrate our training program with the national church. Its pace should be synchronized with the tempo of the national church, and its program should be such that it will truly meet the needs of the church. There is a tendency for institutions to become an end in themselves instead of a means to an end. Sometimes missionaries feel that the Bible school is their particular sphere of influence, and they carry on quite independently of the national church. However, it is the national church that is to furnish the students, and it is the national church that is to be served. The church should feel that the training program is their own and that the trained workers produced are their own workers, not the mission's.

Third, the workers should be trained to the task, not away from it! Some institutions seem to have for an objective the sealing off of the student from his ordinary life. The directors seem to feel that it is necessary to separate the student and infuse in him the school spirit and build his character under the direct supervision of the school in order that he may be properly prepared for the work which he is to do. Probably there are some advantages, but it is difficult to know how a student that is kept in an artificial climate of a theological school for three years or more can make the proper adjustment to the demands of rugged pioneer work when his schooling is finished. The New Testament approach is more along the line of on-the-job training. Jesus taught His disciples, but He took them with Him. When He said, "Look on the fields; the harvest truly is great," He was in the midst of visible need. The harvest field was not something found on a missionary map of the world, but was rather portrayed in the needs of the sick and sinful that were surrounding them on every side. Jesus taught His disciples, and then sent them out to preach and to heal the sick. When they were confronted with failures, as in the case of the man with a lunatic son, He gave further instruction. He taught them on the job. In Acts 19 Paul had a training school in Ephesus where he taught for two full years. Lest anyone think this was classroom instruction only, read the following statement that "so all Asia heard the Word of the Lord." Certainly Paul himself did not take this message personally to all Asia. He taught, and with on-the-job training, the workers and elders that were raised up under his ministry were the messengers that accomplished this tremendous task of evangelism.

Fourth, we must provide for the training of the en-

tire church rather than the exclusive training of a select few who will be devoting themselves to full-time
ministry. We must in our training fill in the artificial
gap that seems to exist between clergy and laity. The
whole church functions as the body of Christ with every
individual Christian having his place and his ministry.
Certainly all are not called to be preachers or teachers,
but all are called to work for God. The whole church
is a functioning organism. How far we have drifted
from this in our churches in America and, therefore,
how difficult it is for us to inaugurate a New Testament
pattern on the foreign field! We tend to give training
only to some who will become ministers, thus sadly
neglecting the entire body of Christ, the army of witnesses that God intends to bring the gospel to every
creature. Can we let such immense manpower go to
waste and still expect to succeed in our task?

Jesus not only sent out the twelve but "other seventy
also." What place do we have for the "other seventy
also" in our present training program? The New Testament church had not only the apostles but, when these
stayed in Jerusalem after the persecution which came
at the death of Stephen, the *disciples* were scattered
abroad and went everywhere preaching the Word. I believe that we are missing a tremendous opportunity for
the kingdom by failing to develop a lay ministry. Ordinarily training programs are set up in such a way that
only the younger people can attend. Those who have
family responsibilities find no way to meet these responsibilities and get the necessary training. Often,
too, insufficient provision is made for those who do not
have the necessary schooling to prepare them to carry
the heavier studies. I believe that the church has the
obligation to provide training for everyone that God is
calling. It does not have to be the same degree of training for all; rather, teaching should be tailored to fit the
need of each class. Remember too that the worker is
not required to have all of the knowledge available before he begins to work. It is necessary for the one that

teaches to be only one step ahead of those who are taught. The new convert can witness to the unsaved, and older converts can help the new converts. The pastor can help the deacons and local workers; the missionaries and Bible school instructors can help the pastors. Converts can become Sunday school teachers; Sunday school teachers can become lay workers; lay workers can become pastors. If all birds refused to sing because they could not equal the nightingale, the forest would be a silent place.

When a farmer is harvesting a fruit crop, he not only needs a truck with a driver, but for each truck he needs several men with baskets who will handpick the fruit and bring it to the truck. There is no advantage in multiplying the number of trucks and truck drivers above the amount of pickers who will in turn fill the trucks. This is a rather crude illustration of the importance of the lay preacher. We have concentrated on the training of the "driver"; we need to give more attention to getting more "pickers" out on the field.

Fifth, we must not neglect the older converts. In New Testament times, the church laid hold of the more mature elements among the converts and these became the church elders. Some had ministry in the Word and others helped govern the work. Let us see what we can find in favor of this arrangement.

It is the biblical pattern. Can we really improve on the model given us in the New Testament? Do we not subject the work to grave dangers and weaknesses when we substitute a system of our own (even though time-honored and widely followed) for the New Testament method?

These men are recognized as men of mature judgment by their own people and are their natural leaders. Thus there is no question of leadership being thrust upon the local congregation by a foreign missionary.

These elders know their own people and are schooled in the wisdom of their own race. It is true that they will carry on things in their own way rather than in the American way, but is not this necessary if the church is to be truly indigenous?

The growth in the Christian ministry of such an elder will be natural rather than forced. The people of the community will think of him as one of their own number, rather than as a professional Christian employee of a foreign mission. His influence will be proportionately greater. The elder will grow into the ministry as a result of normal Christian development, and his growth will not be a "hothouse" growth fostered in a mission station. His zeal to work for God will be the result of his spiritual experience. His desire will be to make Christ known and he will be happy for an opportunity to preach in outstations and surrounding villages. When he is given Bible training, it will be because he *is* a gospel worker; not in the hope that training will make him one.

He will be already established in business or farming; therefore the missionary will not have to support him. The day should come when the local church will assume his support in order to free him for full-time service, but he will always be largely free from the fault, so common to mission-trained workers, of looking to the missionary for the supply of his financial needs.

These elders introduce a mature element in the administration of church affairs. They represent a national Christian leadership, thus providing a stabilizing influence in the government of the church. Moreover, their decisions will be formed from the national point of view—an indispensable factor in the building of a strong national church. This factor is entirely lacking when missionaries make the decisions which in turn must be accepted without question by mission-trained workers.

In Nicaragua a man was converted at the age of fifty-eight. Desirous of serving God, he entered Bible school at the age of sixty. After his studies there, he served a Nicaraguan church as pastor for fifteen years. We must not overlook men like him. If we train only young men because we can mold them and give them a complete theological education, we shall retard the development of the national church.

J. Herbert Kane comments,

> All things being equal, a man with a college education is better than one without. Naturally we missionaries would like to see some seminary men join the work in North Anhwei; but experience has taught us that these people do not always turn out well. They invariably have difficulty in adjusting themselves to the primitive conditions existing in the interior. Having once become accustomed to a semi-western style of living in Shanghai or Hong Kong, they are unable, many of them, to "eat bitterness" along with the uncouth people of the country districts. Sooner or later they fall sick, or grow weary in well-doing, and drift to the larger cities, which offer more scope for their talents and better opportunity for advancement. Local men with a moderate amount of schooling have no such trouble. Having been brought up in the district they are part of the community. They are familiar with local customs; they speak the local dialect; and they eat the local food. Moreover, their shops and homes are there. Their farms and families are there. This gives stability to their work, and stability always makes for permanency.[1]

It may be objected that elders with so little training cannot be trusted to do things in the proper way, Yet, the Apostle Paul trusted them. It is doubtless true that they will make mistakes, but the missionary himself makes mistakes even after years of service. Probably the real objection is that the missionary feels that this type of worker introduces an element into the work over which he has very little control. But is this a bad thing? We cannot have missionary-dominated workers and a strong national church at the same time. Paul commended the elders and the churches "to the Holy Ghost." Cannot we trust the same Holy Spirit to give

[1] J. Herbert Kane, *Twofold Growth*, pp. 156-57.

true leadership to the local churches through their own elders? May God increase our faith!

Adapt Bible Training to the Field

Of course, some very real problems present themselves in training these more mature men for leadership. Young men can leave their homes for extended periods of time to receive Bible training, while the older men are tied down with family and business obligations. At least some of the difficulty arises from the fact that missionaries are given to patterning their Bible-training program after the Bible institute or seminary in the homeland, instead of adapting it to the needs of the field. Sometimes, too, natural love of institutions causes the missionary to permit the institution to become an end in itself. He is actually striving to make the Bible school a great institution instead of merely using it as a tool for attaining a greater end: the development of the national church. If our present methods are not helping us to reach our goal of a strong indigenous church, then those methods should be revised or discarded.

Accessibility of the Bible school is a point of importance. Within certain limits, we should put accessibility to the student first and convenience to the missionary second. Of course, such matters as climate and health, both for the student and missionary, must influence the decision as to locality. In an agricultural community, seedtime and harvest must also be taken into account so that the farm workers may be able to attend. Most of the people are very poor and, since we do not intend to assume their support, we should not inaugurate a program that would deprive them of their only opportunity of making a living. In a city it may be necessary to limit the training program to night classes. We should be versatile enough to meet the demands of changing circumstances.

ADVANTAGES OF SHORT SCHOOL TERMS

Then the *length of the course* must be considered. In Central America we have found that if we are to keep the mature men coming to Bible training school, four months is about as long as we can hold one course. Some have urged upon us the regular eight- or nine-month term, but we found if we did this that our older men with families could not come.

Mature students will have to make some provision for their families. Some of them are pastors of small churches. If they do not come from too great a distance, they can return to care for their families and churches over weekends. But if the term is too long, they are unable to bear the financial strain. And the worker is unable to care for his church. For that reason we have kept the school term short.

Another advantage of a short training course is that there is less danger of overloading the student with knowledge beyond his spiritual capacity. Training should keep pace with spiritual development. When knowledge exceeds spiritual growth, we develop a superficial worker— a man long on theory and ability but short on experience in Christian living. It is better to give a man four months of study and eight months to work out in his life and ministry the knowledge gained, than to give him eight or nine months of study at one time with only a short vacation before beginning another term. The student does not have sufficient opportunity to absorb the knowledge already received and put theory into practice. After finishing one course of four months' study, students often skip a year. This is a distinct advantage, for when the worker does come back to school he has much greater capacity to receive new instruction. Consequently he gets much more help from the course than if he had attended without interruption.

Decentralized Training Program

There is a real advantage in having a *decentralized training program*. The school can then be carried to the districts and it is not necessary to depend entirely upon students coming to the central location. The nearer we can keep our training program to the source of workers (the local churches), the more effective it will be. Perhaps there is no better method for strengthening the churches of a district than to take a short course of Bible studies to one of the central churches of the area. These short annual courses may be from one week to one month in duration. Deacons, lay workers and Sunday school teachers, together with other Christians desirous of engaging in Christian service, gather from nearby churches for classes every day during this period.

Food is contributed by offerings from the churches and perhaps a small quota is paid by each student. Thus we can give the students training right in the very locality in which they are to work.

Those attending this short course have their appetite whetted for a more complete course of studies in the regular Bible school. If practical evangelism is carried on at the same time, the short course serves as a stimulus to all the churches in the area.

In Central America, regular first-year courses are given in each of the republics to provide elementary training for lay preachers and aspirants to the ministry.[2] Eventually, as a sufficient number of national teachers develops, the complete course may be given in each republic. In this way, decentralization of the Bible-training program hastens the evangelization of each republic and the development of workers.

In recent times an interesting experiment has been made by a group in Latin America (UNICO-Unión de los Institutos Bíblicos de la Gran Colombia) which has

[2]The Central American republics are so small that each one would correspond to a province in larger countries.

seen the need for training pastors and prospective workers by means of an extension program which reaches the student on his own level and in his own home without necessity of his going to a regular Bible institute. Each student studies his lessons, aided by a workbook. He is visited periodically by an instructor who reviews the work done and makes new assignments. This method has proved successful to a degree, at least, in areas where local circumstances were such that the regular Bible institute or seminary program had not produced the desired results.

The *course of studies* given in the Bible school should be arranged to meet the needs of the field, taking into account local problems, customs and the religious views of the community. It is usually not sufficient merely to duplicate or translate Bible study courses from Bible schools in the homeland. Often these courses must be simplified or revised in order that the students may receive maximum benefit.

It is well for the missionary who plans to teach in a Bible school to get practical experience in the country by close contact with the people in their everyday life. He should acquire firsthand knowledge of the problems peculiar to the area before he undertakes a teaching ministry. If, on the other hand, he endeavors to give advice on problems when he is still unfamiliar with the background, he is almost certain to make serious blunders. An intimate knowledge of the people is a prerequisite for the training of workers.

TRAIN BY ASSOCIATION

Let the missionary remember that his personal association with the workers is a most important factor in their training. Jesus took disciples with Him. Let the missionary travel with his workers on foot, on horseback, by truck, train or bus as the opportunity affords. Let him eat with them at the same table and at night share the same room. Questions of all categories will be brought up—doctrinal, social and personal. The worker will learn much from the missionary's words, but more from his attitudes. Through such contacts the missionary gains opportunities of imparting not only his knowledge but also his own spirit and vision.

The goal is to develop not only pastors for local congregations, but leaders also for every ministry that the church will need. Evangelistic, teaching and executive abilities must be developed. God gives the gift of government, the word of knowledge and the word of wisdom to various men among the converts. The church must have these men, and the missionary needs vision to detect and select them from among the converts, and patience to develop them so that they can fulfill their calling.

Train for Teaching and Executive Positions

The Bible school and the churches need teachers, so the missionary must thrust the responsibility of teaching upon men who have a budding gift along that line. The church needs national executives to help solve difficult problems and provide adequate leadership for advancement. Again the missionary must thrust the responsibility for decision upon these men—withdrawing himself from the scene—and leave the responsibility upon their shoulders for increasingly long periods of time. Everyone learns by doing. There is no other way of developing teachers and leaders than for the missionary to prepare men as best he can by teaching, and then put them to work, even though they are not yet fully capable of performing the task. If we insist that men must be fully capable before we trust them with responsibility, we shall never be ready to let go of the reins of government.

Free and Open Discussion

In the development of leadership, whether pastors or officials who will hold a position in the national organization, it is important that both missionaries and nationals understand the value of free and open discus-

sion in arriving at decisions and solving problems. We
have all seen good men in a position of leadership who,
because they failed to consult with their associates,
have been a disappointment to their fellow workers.
Their administration failed for lack of coordination and
cooperation.

> In an indigenous work the brethren need not only
> Bible teaching, they also must learn how to deal with
> the administrative and other problems which are essen-
> tially bound up with the life of the church . . . for the
> missionary to decide these matters for them either by
> imposing his fiat or by the subtler method of discus-
> sions to approve his wish, is to hinder the develop-
> ment of the native brethren. They need to be awakened
> to the nature of the problem so that they may appre-
> ciate the solution and perceive how to apply it to their
> own varying conditions, and this awakening comes only
> through one and another discussing the matter from
> his viewpoint and circumstances. . . . The democratic
> method of free decision after full discussion is not in-
> fallible, but neither is the dictatorial fiat. On the
> other hand, it has the very great merits of decision
> by the natives, who know their people and customs;
> of readier acceptance and support; of correction if
> mistaken; and, above all, of educating the constituency
> in the matters of government. Without this there can-
> not be a truly indigenous church.[3]

Some missionaries have shown a reluctance to place
themselves on common ground with the nationals in
meeting a problem. They have felt that to ask advice is
to lower their position in the eyes of the workers. This
is a mistaken attitude, not only because the missionary
thus deprives himself of the valuable contribution that
the nationals can make to him in correctly interpreting
their own people and problems, but also because he
misses an excellent opportunity to instruct the workers
by his own example in the process of solving problems
by group discussion and group decision.

[3]John Ritchie, *Indigenous Church Principles in Theory and
Practice*, p. 56.

The missionary should refrain from using the opportunity for discussion to gain his own end by the weight of his argument or by the force of his personality, so that his plan is accepted even when no true agreement has been reached. He must wait for the slower minds to think things through, and *never assume that silence gives consent.* Sometimes even "yes" really means "no," and when the missionary takes a hesitant "yes" to mean that the brethren approve, he is quite likely to find the problem back again within a few days, as unsolved as ever. If we force upon the nationals a decision that is not really their own, they will get out from under the yoke which we have placed upon them at the first opportunity. When we are not there to enforce the decision, it will not be enforced because it was not really theirs. They merely said "yes" to please the missionary, but their heart was not in it.

Patience is required in such discussions. The missionary should refrain from doing all the talking, and draw the brethren out little by little until he really understands their fears and the cause of their reluctance. Even when their remarks seem needlessly long and beside the point, he should allow them to take their verbal excursions. Presently they will make a statement or ask a question that will help him to get at the heart of the matter. Then, and only then, will he be able to guide the brethren to a decision that will truly meet their approval.

Sometimes he may not be able to convince them 100 percent of the correctness of his own opinion. But then, he may not be 100 percent right! Even though he were entirely right, yet it would be better to bring them along with him wholeheartedly half of the way and stop there temporarily, knowing that it had been their decision, than to insist on their going all the way against their own judgment. Later on he may hope to show them the advisability of taking further steps. For the moment, he has made strides toward his goal in that the nationals are making the decisions and in the right direction.

AVOID BYPASSING NATIONAL LEADERS

Having placed men in positions of authority, or having allowed the church to do so, the missionary should be careful not to snatch up the reins of authority again and bypass the national leaders. Probably most missionaries have been guilty of this. As the *Indian Standard* says, "We complain of their lack of independence, and then outvote them whenever they show a spark of it." We teach that the church is to be self-governing, but when some important problem comes up, instead of presenting the matter for the decision of the national leaders, we simply tell them what to do. We disregard their position, set them to one side, and do as we think best. Then they know that although we talk about the nationals taking responsibility and assuming leadership, yet in reality we do not permit it. They know that when a decision of importance is to be made, we will do as we please. Thus they not only fail to follow us in our decisions, with a corresponding lack of coordination in the work, but resentments may develop and schisms form between nationals and missionaries.

As the missionary by precept and example teaches both the value of group discussion and group decision, he prepares the nationals for the time when the full responsibility shall be left in their own hands. Thus each one learns that he is not to decide important questions on his own individual responsibility, but that major decisions are reached and policies laid down after full and open discussion with his brethren. This will be a safeguard in administration and for the church as a whole.

6

SELF-SUPPORT

Self-support is not necessarily the most important aspect of the indigenous church, but it is undoubtedly the most discussed. In fact, some speak as though a self-supporting church were identical with an indigenous church. We have already pointed out that this is not the case, for a congregation may be able to support itself and still not have initiative for evangelism or the ability to govern itself.

It is regrettable that the use of money by the missionary has often weakened rather than strengthened the church. The right use of money has its place in the missionary program but, if missionaries were to be faced with the choice of too much money or too little, it would probably be better for the church if the missionaries chose too little. When the missionary does not have money, he must depend on God and encourage national initiative. There are self-supporting works in existence today, due not so much to the wisdom of the missionary as to the fact that he had very limited financial resources and could not offer financial help to national workers. Later he realized that what he had supposed was a hindrance to the work was in reality a boon. A vigorous national church had been established.

DANGERS IN USE OF FUNDS

Missionaries who make appeals asking for money to support national workers or to erect church buildings, etc., should carefully weigh the long-range consequences and be sure that their procedure will truly strengthen the church, not weaken it. The future of the church should not be sacrificed for the sake of temporary advantage. Missionaries who plead for funds, asking for foreign help to do for the national church that which it should rightfully do for itself, should examine their position to see if they are on scriptural ground. Sometimes we get the impression that the missionary believes that the work of the Holy Spirit depends on the amount of money available. The Word of the Lord is not bound; it is we who are "straitened" in our own vision and understanding.

E. Gideon writes:

> I have kept to the last what seems to me the most serious indictment of the work of the Church. Most of the churches in India are not self-supporting. This is a very serious matter. Analyzed critically, it means this: Indian Christians take their religion so lightly and superficially that they are not prepared to contribute adequately to the support of their own churches and their own ministers. I do not know of any community outside India which would permit of such a state of affairs. And missions and missionaries acquiesce in this, nay, encourage it by soliciting more and more money from abroad. But it seems to me that so long as Indians are not prepared to sacrifice whatever is necessary to support their churches, this is convincing proof that the church has failed in its fundamental objective—to convince a people of the truth of Christianity, for surely it is true in this, as in all ages of all peoples in all countries, that the only real test of conviction is the desire and willingness to sacrifice.
>
> It is a shameful thing that we cannot stand comparison in this matter with our Hindu and Muslim brethren. I think we have a right to ask the missions why they have allowed things to come to such a pass, why they have so pauperized and weakened us that the indigenous church instead of being a sturdy, virile, self-reliant body, able and willing to be self-sufficient, is a

feeble, weedy, top-heavy administration, the members of which are always turning to the West with imploring eyes, and abject, outstretched hands asking for alms. In this, I maintain the church has failed in its most important work, and the measure of its material success in obtaining foreign men and foreign money is the exact measure of its spiritual failure in this country.

At a gathering of the Evangelical Foreign Missions Association, Rev. T. Stanley Soltau of Korea made this statement: "I am convinced that the amount of foreign feeling can nearly always be expected in exact proportion to the amount of foreign funds used. The more foreign funds used in the work, the more anti-foreign sentiment you are likely to have."

There is no doubt that the use of money by the missionary has been the cause of much resentment on the part of the nationals. The nationals do not understand the missionary's point of view; they think that he is not as generous as he should be, or that he is partial in his treatment of the workers. They may feel that the missionary uses the power which the distribution of funds places in his hands as a lever to get his own way. It is hard to get around the idea that the man who holds the purse strings is the boss. The real mistake in all this has been in teaching the converts to look to the missionary as a source of income.

REASONS FOR SELF-SUPPORT

The church on the mission field should be self-supporting for the following reasons:

First, it is the Bible plan. If this were the only reason for insisting on self-support, it would be sufficient. A reading of the Acts of the Apostles will convince anyone that this was the apostolic method. We find no hint that the churches among the Gentiles were supported by the Jewish congregation. Instead, we do find that the Apostle Paul solicited offerings from the churches he had founded to help relieve the distress among the famine-stricken saints in Jerusalem (Acts 24:17; Rom. 15:26). A striking contrast to today's procedure!

Tithing Is the Bible Method

We accept tithing as a scriptural basis for the support of the work in the homeland, believing that they who preach the gospel should live of the gospel. Circumstances may differ but the principle is the same everywhere. Why not apply it the world around?

Second, it is a logical plan. Under ordinary circumstances, even the poorest can support a pastor according to their own standard of living if there are ten or more faithful tithing families in the congregation. Some missionaries object on the ground that the people are too poor to support their pastor. They overlook the fact that these same people once supported their priests or witchdoctors in heathendom. Strangely enough, one missionary contended that the converts on his field were *too well off* to support their pastor! I had pointed out that the Christians on a certain field were very poor, the daily wage a mere pittance, yet they supported their own pastors. He informed me that this was possible because the people in the area were accustomed to poverty. "But our people are different," he reasoned, "they come from a higher class and we could not expect a pastor to live on what the people would give him."

Of course, if we introduce an American standard of living, it will require the equivalent of an American income to support the work. If we consider the preaching of the gospel as a profession, then it is logical that the pastor must live as a doctor or lawyer; and his support would be beyond the reach of a poor congregation. But if we follow the New Testament pattern, in which the pastor is one with his flock, and lives on the same level as the members of his congregation, then there is no reason why ten families who support themselves, cannot also support a pastor with their tithes.

Third, the spiritual welfare of the congregation de-

mands that it be self-supporting. A sense of responsibility fosters spiritual blessings. Deprive the converts of the privilege of giving and the responsibility of sacrificing to support the work, and weak Christians will result. They will likely be inactive also in evangelism and fail to assume the responsibility of church discipline. They will be willing to allow the missionary to do everything. On the other hand, they cherish a work which has cost them sacrifice and effort.

Take church property as an illustration. In one city the mission had furnished everything that the congregation needed when the work began. Land, building and benches were all provided, and the congregation had the use of this property for more than twenty years.

I visited there during a period when there was no resident missionary in the district. The congregation called my attention to the state of the building and asked help for even the simplest repairs. We might ask, "Well, brethren, since you have had the use of this building for twenty years, isn't it time that you assume the cost of these repairs?" But they do not see it that way. The property belongs to the mission, and one does not repair other people's property.

In the same country a new work was started. After a few months it became imperative to secure a property where the little group of converts could meet. We got together the funds that were available and the pastor secured a small loan; but it still was not enough. As we studied the situation, one of the brethren said, "I think that I can give so much more for this need." Another said, "I, too, will give the same amount." Seeing that they were doing their best, I made a personal offering also. The property was secured and the pastor and his little congregation went to work. They repaired the building inside and out. They laid a cement floor to take the place of the dirt one. After a few months it was a much better building than when it was purchased. The sense of responsibility and ownership made the difference.

CONGREGATIONS SHOULD ERECT THEIR CHAPELS

Some of our congregations in Central America have struggled for ten years to build their chapel. They have begun in a private home, moved into a thatch-roofed hut of their own and finally, after years of sacrifice and labor, have completed their frame or adobe building. Their little chapel means infinitely more to them than if it had been provided by the mission.

A missionary, William Shillingsburg, tells in the publication, *The Pilot,* about one section of Colombia where fifteen missionaries are stationed:

At least one hundred and fifty preaching points are visited each month. Over one-third of these centers have built their own place of worship, leaving of course the majority of the services to be held in private homes. The twenty-five part-time and full-time native preachers, who make monthly rounds, receive no salary but support themselves (and in some cases their families) by manual labor and the small offerings their people give them.

"But let us ask: How many churches or school buildings would the native Christians have built if the mission had started doing it for them? Answer: None. When would the native church grow to support their own pastors if the mission would do it for them? Answer: Never.

The native church left to its own, of course has to suffer; it has to struggle and sometimes its efforts seem so feeble, we feel sorry and want to help. The result, however, would be the same as the effect produced by the preacher who helped what would have become a beautiful butterfly from its cocoon. He watched impatiently the great and seemingly futile effort to emerge, until his good but misunderstanding heart could stand it no longer; so with his sharp penknife he cut a few of the silken cords at the mouth of the encasement. Struggling ceased and there burst forth— a shapeless, weak, helpless, ugly mass to live but a moment. . . . A rule of life had been violated. Left to itself, after much writhing, contortion and labor, a well-formed, strong and beautifully colored creature would have come forth. . . . A bamboo house with a straw roof and mud walls, built with native money and full of people is better than a beautiful brick and cement structure built with foreign funds that has but a half-dozen in the congregation. . . .

No, money for native preachers and native churches is not a handicap nor hindrance; it is a challenge to missionary ability, and a policy that, if adopted generally and more rigidly, would save many a heartache and produce a stronger, more humble church in the foreign field.

Fourth, the pastor needs to feel that his responsibility is to his congregation rather than to the mission. Quite naturally the mission-paid worker is responsible to the mission paying his salary. As long as he has the approval of the missionary, he has nothing to fear. The pastor who is not supported by the mission, but chosen and maintained by the congregation, feels his responsibility to his flock. The congregation will also feel a closer tie with its pastor. The pastor will see that if he is to better his condition, even financially, he must build up his church. This interdependence is most salutary for both pastor and church.

MISSION SUPPORT WEAKENS WORKERS

Fifth, the spirit of faith and sacrifice required on the part of the worker helps develop a vigorous spiritual ministry. It is spiritually healthy for the pastor to be obliged to trust God for his support. The missionary can stunt a worker's spiritual growth by depriving him of the necessity of depending upon God. A worker is not likely to develop that rugged and robust character, so necessary to a spiritual ministry, if the missionary constantly defends him from the struggle by supplying his needs. The mission-supported worker learns to bring each new financial problem to the missionary. He is the source of his income. When he marries, when a baby is born, when there is illness, he comes to present his need to the missionary. This cannot but have a withering effect on the worker's moral and spiritual character.

Workers who are lacking in the faith and stamina required by the rigors of a life of dependence upon God will soon eliminate themselves from the list of workers. Under the system of mission support, they might continue drawing their salary for years, and thus constitute an element of spiritual weakness in the church.

We have found a fairly accurate "Gideon's test" to distinguish between those who are truly called of God, and those who lack that call. Any effort through financial means to hold a worker, who without financial help would not continue in the ministry, is certain to weaken the indigenous church. What is more, it hinders the spiritual growth of the worker himself.

States one missionary:

> Pastors receiving outside aid have in many instances grown lazy and remained aloof from the financial problems of their churches. An instance: A pastor who had been receiving foreign assistance was asked to take charge of two small church groups, thereby receiving aid from both churches and attaining a fair degree of financial independence from foreign funds. This pastor thought the matter over for a while, rather disliked the extra work involved in caring for two churches instead of one, and finally wrote a letter refusing to care for more than one church. From this one instance, which could be multiplied many times, it can be observed that the continued acceptance of foreign assistance kills even evangelistic incentive.

Sixth, in the end the worker is better off financially without mission support. When a worker receives even a portion of his support from the mission, it almost invariably means that the members of his congregation will not assume the proper responsibility for his support. They consider that he receives a salary. It may be that he actually receives only one-third of the amount that he needs, yet it is enough to keep them from feeling personally responsible.

The funds that a mission has at its disposal for the support of national workers are usually limited and, as a result, are spread out too thinly to care adequately for the workers. As a result, the worker fails to receive sufficient support either from the mission or from his congregation. When some of our national workers have been cut off completely from the help of the mission, and their congregations have become aware that they are entirely responsible for the support of their pastor, the workers have found that in not too long a time their income is better than when they were subsidized by the mission.

Also there is likely to be better feeling between the worker and the missionary. Usually the allowances are not adequate, and so, as the worker suffers he may unconsciously build up resentment against the missionary, feeling that he should do something to relieve his distress. But when the worker ceases to consider the missionary as an employer and recognizes his own ministry as a God-given responsibility, his whole outlook toward the work and the missionary is favorably affected.

Seventh, self-support places the national worker in an advantageous position with his countrymen. Mission-paid workers have been accused of being spies for a foreign power, and the monthly check has been used as evidence against them. Some workers have been put to death or are in concentration camps because of this. As the spirit of nationalism grows, and propaganda increases against "Yankee imperialism," we shall need increasingly to safeguard our national workers and churches against the possibilities of such false accusations. In Latin America the priests often tell the people that missionaries are paid by Wall Street, and are the forerunners of political and economic domination by the "Colossus of the North." Naturally, then, mission-paid workers may easily be considered agents of a foreign power. When one of our missionaries had occasion to explain to an official of the American embassy in his country that our churches are self-governing and self-supporting, this man remarked: "I am delighted to hear this. If all missions would work on that principle it would save our department a good many headaches."

Even when a mission-paid worker is not accused of being a political agent of a foreign power, he may still be considered the agent of a foreign religion, preaching a foreign doctrine because he is paid for it. His countrymen will question his sincerity.

Writing of North Africa, J. J. Cooksey declares:

> The day of big things [for Christianity] . . . will come, if ever, when Islam can see men, members of its own household, who, undirected by an alien Western organization, unpaid by foreign missionary funds, will spend themselves and their all for their faith, and be ready to seal it with their blood. . . . The employed native Christian agent makes the Moslem smile in his beard; the foreign missionary he indulgently tolerates. He will only furiously think . . . when Christ really and utterly captures some Moslem heart in sacrificial power, fills it with His Spirit, and consecrates it for the task of building an indigenous North African Christianity.[1]

To understand how the receiving of a salary paid from foreign funds affects a Christian worker's standing in the eyes of his compatriots, let us reverse the picture. How would we feel about one of our neighbors who would receive a salary from some Moslem mission of Arabia to distribute literature and make converts for Islam among us? Would we be deeply convinced of his sincerity? On the other hand, the man who from deep conviction and at the cost of great personal sacrifices preaches his doctrine without remuneration from a foreign source has no such handicap to overcome.

Eighth, self-support opens the door to unlimited expansion. One of the most discouraging aspects of depending on foreign funds for the support of pastors and churches is that it automatically limits the church's capacity for extension. For example, if a missionary re-

---

[1] J. J. Cooksey, *In the Land of the Vanished Church*, pp. 54-55.

ceives $100 monthly for the work in his area, it will not
be long until every cent of it will be allocated. From
then on every new worker places an additional strain on
the budget. Every new church requires additional
funds. The missionary appeals for extra help so that
he can enter the open doors before him, but the mission
board must reply that funds are not available. Such a
notice is equivalent to saying, "Do not open any more
outstations, or found any more churches. Do not encourage any more converts to enter the ministry. We
cannot provide the funds for additional activities."
Surely God would not place His messenger in such a
ridiculous predicament. This situation is avoided when
the missionary does not depend on foreign funds for
the maintenance of the work. The indigenous church
has no such limitations placed upon it, for it draws
from the country itself and, as it expands, finds within
itself the means for its own support.

THE "HOW" OF SELF-SUPPORT

Having summarized the principal factors that make
the self-support of the national church imperative, we
shall see how this goal may be attained.

If we are to attain self-support, it is important that
we lay the right foundation from the very beginning of
the work, since the procedures we establish with the
first few converts in founding the first church, will
doubtless become the pattern to be followed by the converts and churches which will spring up later in the district.

It may be objected that if we start mentioning money
at the very beginning, we shall make a bad impression
on the people. In Latin America, for example, the priests
are always asking for money, so, in order to prove that
the Protestants are different, some missionaries and
national workers have gone to the other extreme. They
never mention the question of finance or take up an
offering, at least in the first months or even years of the
work. The fact that the subject has been abused does

not free us from our obligation to give the correct teaching and establish wholesome practices.

It is much easier to teach a convert his financial obligations to the work of God during the first few weeks after his conversion than it is to do so after he has been a member of the church for ten years. He will see no reason why he should begin then, after he has enjoyed the privilege of salvation and membership for so long without it. So the time to start is while the converts are still young in the faith. If their lives have received the touch of the Spirit of God, they will respond to the challenge of carrying their own proper share of the load.

TEACH CONVERTS TO TITHE

Converts should know what is to be expected of them before they are accepted as members of the church. Teach the new converts that they should pay tithes, even before they are baptized in water. There is no advantage in accepting converts as members of the church who have no intention of fulfilling the duties of an ordinary Christian. Let us not be afraid that they will slip away if we teach them their responsibilities. It is better to build a little more slowly and lay a proper foundation than to build more quickly and find out afterward that the work cannot progress for lack of a proper beginning. Once the foundation is laid, the growth will be solid and the benefits of the increased blessings upon the work will more than repay for the time required to give the necessary teaching at the beginning.

Sometimes the enthusiasm with which the converts respond to an appeal surprises us. We have seen them enter into the spirit of hilarious giving, donating land, labor and materials for church buildings. Churches have given hundreds of pounds of corn and beans for the support of Bible students, and others have given the "widow's mite" in their poverty, sacrificing literally all they have in order to see the work of God prosper. The liberality of these converts has been a source of amazement to visitors. God honors faith, and we need to believe that He will work in the hearts of His people along the line of self-support, just as we believe that His Spirit will stir up the believers to respond to any other phase of gospel truth. Here, as elsewhere in the spiritual realm, the law is "according to your faith be it unto you."

PIONEER WORKERS SUPPORT THEMSELVES

In a pioneer work, unless the national evangelist receives help from neighboring churches, it may be necessary for him to find some secular employment until the church is fully established. Of course, a full-time ministry is better as a worker is then free to give more time to his spiritual task. But a minister who must work temporarily with his hands to support himself and his family, is to be preferred to one who is dependent on foreign funds for his support. The example of the Apostle Paul can be safely followed in this case (Acts 20:35; 18:3).[2]

Probably the standard procedure followed by most missionaries in opening a work in a new town is open to

[2]A word of caution should be given. While it is commendable for a worker to support himself by secular employment during the pioneer stages of a work, yet it is harmful for the worker to continue to do so after the church is established. Then his sacrifice is not a blessing but a hindrance, for the congregation is permitted to shirk its rightful responsibility. This results in the loss of spiritual blessing and vision. The church is robbed of the fruits of a full-time ministry. Furthermore, it will be difficult for any other worker to follow in the pastorate, since the congregation probably will demand that he, too, support himself.

The ministry of the worker is adversely affected also. Robbed of time for study and prayer, he is unable to "feed the flock." He has little time for visiting his members. Tired after a day's work in the field or shop, he cannot give his best to the midweek services. The whole church suffers.

Then, too, secular work may become a snare to a worker, tempting him to leave the ministry entirely. It has happened!

Every established church should support its own pastor. Workers should be encouraged to devote their full time to the ministry from the time that the church is set in order.

criticism. The accepted method seems to be to pick out a town that needs a church, then rent a hall, furnish it with seats, etc., hang up a sign, and start preaching services. The first night's audience will likely be composed mostly of children. These disappear after the priest (in Latin America) has visited the parents and told them to keep their children away from services.

Thus prejudice is built up from the very beginning. The missionary is a foreigner, preaching a foreign religion. The cost of everything is paid by him. Later on, when converts are won, they will see no reason for taking over the financial responsibility for the work. From the beginning the missionary has supplied everything. Why should he not continue to do so?

To avoid these mistakes, it is better that the missionary get acquainted with the people of the vicinity before starting to preach in a designated place of worship. Let him make friends with the neighbors. In their homes he may introduce them to songs or choruses and explain the Scriptures without any formal religious service. Then when interest is sufficient to require a public service, the missionary can suggest that one of those interested open up his home.

It is preferable not to begin regular meetings in the missionary's own home. He may explain that the neighbors will be much more willing to come to another's home than to his own. Someone may offer his front room, or all may go together to rent a large room which can accommodate the people. In such circumstances, they will all feel the responsibility of sharing expenses.

As the missionary travels over the district, visiting towns and villages, he will be constantly on the lookout for people who are friendly to the gospel message. He will endeavor to establish services in their homes. This method is fruitful for the missionary, and even better for the national worker, since the people come to accept their responsibility for the work, and are not likely to consider the missionary or worker as a source of financial aid. Following this plan, it is possible to open up work in a town without resorting to the initiative-killing expedient of having the mission pay all the bills and permitting the new converts to become accustomed to mission support.

OPENING NEW WORK ILLUSTRATED

The following account illustrates this point:

One of our missionaries . . . began a new church in the village of her residence. . . . The first problem that faced her was a meeting place. The small handful of Christians naturally looked to the missionary's residence, for it was perhaps more commodious than any of their homes. The missionary, however, said, "No." They must provide a place for themselves. This seemed harsh and unsympathetic, but it drove the Christians to become resourceful and to consider the solution of their problems without the benefit of the missionary and the missionary's resources. They found a place and therefore the transition from the missionary's home to another place was never necessary. Had they begun to meet in the home of the missionary, they would have been satisfied to stay there indefinitely. Today these Christians have not only rented their church building, but have begun to build their own place of worship.

The next problem was chairs for use during the service. No Christian had enough chairs in his home, so they immediately turned to the missionary. . . . Again the missionary said "No." It did look as though the missionary was not willing to share, but it was a problem for which the church must find a solution, and it did.

The next item that came up for consideration was a light for the evening meetings. They used very small lamps or wicks burning in dishes of oil. These lights, of course, are only good for a general breaking of the darkness in a room or for one individual to use in reading. Again they turned to the missionary, for she had the only adequate light. The missionary gave in and allowed them to use her light. Months passed; in fact a year passed. The missionary's remark is most enlightening: "And who provided the oil for that lamp? The missionary, of course. Did not the lamp belong to the missionary? Therefore the missionary must provide the oil." Thus we see that when the missionary finally did give in . . . this giving in was the entrance for the Christians to use something belonging to the missionary. So until the missionary left, the Christians used not only the lamp but the oil of the missionary.

These things may seem very small. One could condemn the missionary as heartless and indifferent for refusing to share with the Christians. If we investigate further, however, we realize the wisdom of the missionary in insisting that the church depend on its own resources, and to look to itself for the solution of its own problems. Had the missionary opened her house and provided chairs, the time would come when the missionary would leave and the Christians would have been unprepared to assume these simple responsibilities. Not only would they be unprepared, they would still be weak, for whatever the missionary does [in giving financial aid] encourages the Christians to remain "babes" as far as assuming responsibility is concerned. They would not have the privilege of doing things which would strengthen them in their own organic life. The Christians become resourceful and strong in the solution of these matters only as they are given responsibility. The wise move, and in fact the New Testament procedure, is to have the Christians undertake these things themselves from the very beginning.[3]

We would not go so far as to state that there is never a time when foreign funds could be used to help in the work. The guiding principle that must determine whether or not we give funds to a worker or a building project is whether the offering will help to develop a sense of responsibility in the church and workers, or whether it will lessen their initiative. We should never do for others what they ought properly to do for them-

[3]"A Study of Indigenous Policies and Procedures," pp. 14-15, paper of the Conservative Baptist Foreign Missions Society.

selves. Every distribution of financial aid should be judged by this criterion: Will this in the long run help the church to stand on its own feet, or will this make the church more dependent on others?

7

THE NATIONAL ORGANIZATION

Having discussed the establishment of the local church, we will now consider how such churches may be bound together; for the *churches* should become the *church*. In this we are following the New Testament pattern. The Apostle Paul referred to the churches of a province as a unit—as the churches of Macedonia, of Achaia or of Judea (II Cor. 8:1; 9:2; I Thess. 2:14). The same bonds that united the individual Christians in the local church, united these local churches into the church.

CHURCHES NEED TO BE BOUND TOGETHER

Just as individual believers need the fellowship and ministry of other Christians, so the local church needs to recognize that it forms a part of *the* church and especially of that part of the church which is in their own district or province. The necessity for such union arises from the following factors:

First, the need for Christian fellowship. Small groups of individual believers that are cut off from all contact with other churches tend to become discouraged and inactive. Christian fellowship revives the courage of the believers, brings joy in the Holy Spirit and stimulates Christian activity.

Second, Christian unity and fellowship provide a stabilizing and corrective influence upon local congregations. Just as an individual Christian, left to his own devices, may take up strange notions and interpretations of the Scripture, or embrace fanciful or fanatical ideas, so congregations also are open to the same danger. Unity and fellowship tend to correct wrong tendencies. Contact with other churches serves to preserve a spiritual balance in the local congregation.

Third, over-all organization permits the carrying out of specific projects that would be impossible for the local church alone. These projects include the evangelization of unreached sections, the establishing of training centers for Christian workers, and the election and support of qualified overseers, evangelists and teachers who will carry out the projects necessary for the maintenance and advancement of the work.

It has already been pointed out that it is unwise to begin any national organization before there are local churches and national ministers, since any organization that begins with the missionaries will be essentially foreign in character. Americans must not permit their natural love for organization to cause the organization to become an end in itself. The end must always be the establishing and strengthening of the indigenous church, and organization must be kept subservient to that goal.

When there are from three to five churches in a province, it is time to bring representatives of each local church together for fellowship and discussion. In Central America we call these meetings "conferences." In El Salvador the first such gathering had eleven churches represented, but in the other republics, there were not more than four churches established when we called the first "conference."

Geographical features, political boundaries, differences of language and transportation facilities will determine the size of the district to be embraced as a conference or council. There is little to be gained by trying to bind churches together into a single unit when they are far removed from each other and no actual fellowship can be maintained. When distance, language or political barriers make it impractical to unite the

churches into one district, it is advisable to divide the
district into smaller units with a sectional conference
or council in each area.

In much the same way that the charter members of a
local church reach agreement as to the standards for
their local church, so the churches should come together
to discuss the basis for the development of the church
in their area. The local churches are represented by
their pastors and duly elected delegates. Other Christians from the congregations may be present as ob-
servers. These conferences become the annual business
meeting for directing the work of the district.

SECTIONAL PRESBYTERS

As the work extends, the district is divided into sections, with each section having from five to ten local
churches. These churches may meet together in a fellowship meeting every three to six months, as circumstances permit. An overseer or presbyter, chosen at the
annual conference of all the churches, takes the oversight of each section and helps the pastors and churches
in the problems that arise. Since the presbyter is also
a pastor of one of the churches in the section, he will
not need to be supported from other sources. But for
the same reason, the number of churches under his
supervision should be limited in number, or else he will
either neglect his church in caring for the section, or
will be unable to oversee the work properly.

The general officials, such as superintendent, secretary and treasurer, are elected by the general assembly
at the annual meeting. It is probable that the nationals
will desire a missionary to fill the office of superintendent until the nationals are trained in the management of the church. However, as national leaders develop, all official positions should be filled by them.
From the point where the national brethren become
able to fill various offices to the point where they can
take over the entire administration is but a step. It is
best that they do so while there are still missionaries of

experience on the field to guide them. It is poor policy
to wait until the missionaries are suddenly withdrawn
and leadership is forced upon the nationals.

The providing of leadership for the national church
is just as much a part of missionary work as is the win-
ning of converts. To accomplish this, the missionary
must be willing to step aside, working unobtrusively as
the administration passes into the hands of others.

The willingness of the missionary to cooperate with
national leaders is a test both of his humility and of the
quality of his missionary passion. As one national minister expressed it, "Many missionaries are willing to
serve under the District Council [composed of mis-
sionaries] but not under the local committees [with
nationals].... Unless our missionary friends can extri-
cate themselves from this superiority complex, we are
afraid that they will not have much fruitful ministry in
our land."

A SEPARATE ORGANIZATION FOR MISSIONARIES?

Some missions have two organizations for each field:
one composed only of missionaries, the other composed
only of nationals. This may be satisfactory if the missionary organization limits its scope to those matters
which affect missionaries only. But if the missionary
organization is to act as a supreme court and place
limitations on the national organization, reserving the
right of approving or disapproving all resolutions passed
by the nationals, and the power to veto on questions
that affect the churches and the national ministry, then
the system would be liable to a serious breakdown.

I believe that it makes for unity if we have only one
body representing the field; in other words, only one
body with power to make decisions which affect the national work.[1] That body should be composed of repre-

[1]This statement is not intended to discourage the forming of
an organization of missionaries in order to deal with their own
special problems. Such an organization is often a necessity.
However, it should limit its decisions to the sphere of missionary
activity, and not undertake to dictate to the national organization.

sentatives from the local churches, the national ministers and the missionaries. The missionaries may lend
their strength and counsel to the work in the early
stages and even fill executive positions until national
leaders are prepared to take over this responsibility.
Only let the missionary be sure to recognize the proper
time to step aside, permitting the nationals to fill these
posts.

Someone may object: But if the missionaries are allowed a voice in the national organization, they will
completely control it, and there will be, in effect, no
national organization. In such instances, one of the
following circumstances may be to blame, and should
be corrected: *First,* perhaps the work has been organized on a national scale too soon with the missionaries
outnumbering the nationals; *second,* there may be too
many missionaries in that particular area for the good
of the indigenous church (a redistribution of missionary personnel is required), or *third,* something is woe-
fully wanting in the method used to develop the initiative of the workers (the missionaries need to reex-
amine their system).

Since the churches are to have a national organization, some thought must be given to providing financial
support for the officials who will serve them. How this
will be done depends largely upon whether the offices
are considered full-time posts. If not, the superintendent and other officials will retain their pastorates and
will travel over the field to visit the churches only in
special times of need. Ordinary problems can be han-
dled by the presbyter of each section. It must be said
that this plan has much in its favor, inasmuch as it does
not place a financial load upon the churches and tends
to avoid the danger of a top-heavy, overcentralized,
national organization.

On the other hand, experience has taught us that a
tremendous load is often placed upon the official who
must pastor a church and take care of district duties

also; so that the office of superintendent at least is usually a full-time post.

In Central America the pastors support their officials by sending the tithe of their own incomes to the central office. Some conferences augment this through special offerings taken by each church, or by tithing the other church income (outside of that which is given to the support of the pastor), as may be agreed upon by the conference.

8

CONVERTING TO INDIGENOUS CHURCH METHODS

A missionary once remarked, "Starting an indigenous work in a pioneer field is not the major difficulty. What we would most like to know is how to go about converting to indigenous church methods on a field where the work has been carried on for years under the old mission-compound system."

The conversion of a work from a nonindigenous basis to methods which will permit the development of an indigenous church is probably one of the most difficult tasks that a missionary can undertake. Doubtless it would be impossible to make hard and fast rules, adequate for every field. Conditions differ widely. In some places present-day missionaries have fallen heir to a work founded by their predecessors. This work includes a staff of considerable size and a subsidy of mission funds for its support. We can here make only some general suggestions as to possible steps in this conversion, urging at the same time that all missionaries concerned should read books on the subject and study indigenous procedure with a sincere desire to find the proper solution. We trust that the Holy Spirit shall guide both individual missionaries and the administrative staff in taking adequate steps.

Missionaries should not be impatient with nationals who seem slow in changing to the indigenous plan. Rather, they should realize that existing conditions are largely due to wrong training and practice. We must therefore patiently correct our own errors and endeavor to return to the New Testament pattern.

GENERAL PRINCIPLES

In *Twofold Growth* J. Herbert Kane points out that the vast majority of churches on the foreign field have gotten off to a wrong start and that it will not be an easy matter to change after thirty or forty years of practice.

> Our plans, therefore, must be carefully conceived, and wisely executed. In this connection there are three important principles which we must ever bear in mind.
>
> In the first place, *they [the nationals] must be allowed to frame their own policies.* Most missionaries today are in favor of the indigenous church in principle; but when it comes to working out the details they are guilty of . . . back-seat driving. They relinquish the wheel, but they insist on directing the way. This is a very serious mistake. . . .
>
> Secondly, *we must permit them to develop along their own lines* . . . the churches of the East should be allowed to develop their own peculiar type of Christianity. It is not necessary for them to adopt our style of architecture, our order of service, our methods of work, or even our form of government. . . . We must remember that while it is right to make a Christian out of a Moslem, it is wrong to make an American out of a Chinese. . . .
>
> And last, but not least, *they should be allowed to proceed at their own pace.* . . . Many a fine missionary has broken his health and his heart trying to speed up the people of the East. It cannot be done; so the missionary, if he is wise, will come to this conclusion early in his ministry, and thereafter act accordingly. . . . "First the blade, then the ear, after that the full corn in the ear." Our difficulty comes when we want all three in the first ten days. We must be as patient in the building of the church as Jesus was in the training of the twelve. . . . We too must be patient—infinitely

patient—with the church leaders when they fail to
adopt some pet scheme of ours, or when they hesitate
to exercise discipline, or when they omit to send in the
annual report. . . . We must not be surprised if they
are late for the Sunday service, or forget about the
deacons' meeting, or arrive three days late for Bible
school. These are the traits which will require many
years . . . for them to overcome.[1]

As a first step toward conversion to indigenous principles, I would suggest that all the missionaries in the
area gather together for discussion, with the aim of out-
lining a practical plan of procedure. All missionaries
concerned should be present, for it is very important
that there be harmony of spirit and purpose in taking
these steps. Even when all agree as to the ultimate
goal, there still may be sharp differences of opinion as
to the methods to be employed in reaching that goal.
Such differences of opinion may constitute a serious ob-
stacle to the realization of the plan of conversion. Therefore, time spent in prayer and honest discussion in
order to reach agreement is well worthwhile. Patience
must be manifested by all, since it is not easy for a person with years of experience in missionary work to
change his viewpoint or his methods. Plenty of time
should be allowed for a change of thinking to take place.
All the problems will not be solved in one session, nor
perhaps even in one series of sessions. Though progress
seems slow, missionaries may take heart by reminding
themselves that the project is not simply a pet scheme,
but is backed up by the Word of God, and by the Spirit
of God who is certainly leading us in this direction.
He will honor New Testament procedure, direct us in
the steps we should take and enable us to iron out our
differences. So, "if God be for us!"

It may be necessary to make temporary concessions
in order not to disrupt the established work. The un-
known and different factors on each field make it unwise to lay down inflexible rules. Each missionary is a

[1]J. Herbert Kane, *Twofold Growth*, pp. 19-24.

member of Christ's body, and the Holy Spirit will surely guide each one into all truth when there is a sincere desire to do His will. All missionaries will doubtless agree to the proposal that at least all the new work shall be established on indigenous principles. Those missionaries who are desirous of converting the established work can trust that the blessings from the new works will overflow into the established churches. Perhaps then those in charge will see that they are missing great blessings and be more ready to make the change.

INSPIRE NATIONAL WORKERS

Taking it for granted that the missionaries are in favor of following indigenous principles, *the second step* will be to prepare the nationals for the changes to come by showing them the advantages and importance of indigenous methods. Again patient teaching and discussion will be required. As missionaries, we are largely responsible for their viewpoint. We have trained them in dependence upon us; we shall have to retrain them in independence and initiative.

Some missionaries have themselves reached the decision that the work should become indigenous, and have tried to make it so by simply announcing that from that time on, the work was to be self-supporting. They have then precipitately cut off the support of the workers. But there is much more to the problem than merely cutting off a worker from financial support. The initiative for evangelism and leadership must spring from within the national's own spirit. This requires time to develop. It is comparable to the process that changes a boy into a man. The parent instructs, counsels and guides his son, all the while increasing the responsibility upon him and allowing more liberty in decisions until the time comes that the son is capable of making his own way. Contrariwise, we have made the mistake of training the national workers in dependence. We must therefore take steps at once to convert to indigenous principles, but we must give the nationals a period of time in which they may find their own feet. Otherwise they will be left in the difficult circumstance of a boy who suddenly becomes an orphan.

Some of the more fainthearted and less aggressive spirits among the workers may view the idea of conversion to national leadership and responsibility with considerable alarm. Having all their life depended on a salary from the mission, it will require courage and faith to step out without that support. Some workers have been so fearful of being left without the financial backing of the mission that they have failed to adopt the suggestions of the missionary. They have not encouraged the local congregation to do its best in giving for fear that their salary would be cut off.

One missionary relates how the mission, in order to encourage self-support, offered to match the amount given to the pastor by the local congregation up to the maximum of four pounds. Above this amount the foreign funds would be cut back in proportion to increased local offerings.

"Imagine our surprise when in only a month or two practically every pastor had increased local offerings as much as two or three pounds so that he might receive the maximum of foreign matching. . . . Imagine our further surprise as time passed when we observed that these local pastors held their church giving at this peak without endeavoring to carry it on further still to financial independence."

This instance reveals how necessary it is that the nationals shall catch the vision themselves. It will be next to impossible for a missionary to develop a self-supporting church if the worker in charge is not in sympathy with the idea.

However, it is likely that it will be less difficult to convince the nationals of the benefits of the indigenous method than some missionaries suppose. In fact, the missionary may well be surprised at the eagerness with which the nationals grasp the possibilities. As they be-

come inspired with the vision of evangelism through
national initiative and see the opportunities for leadership which a truly indigenous work offers, they will
thrill to the joy of spiritual self-fulfillment. *Most workers will make greater sacrifices and dedicate themselves
more fully to the work of God when inspired by the
opportunity of filling a vital place in the church of God
than they will for the sake of a mere salary.*

Planning for Financial Independence

The third step is to accompany the teaching with appropriate action. The long-range indigenous program
calls for the development of all the ministries which the
church requires—pastors, teachers, evangelists and executives. All must be supplied from among the converts
themselves, and all phases of the national church must
become completely self-supporting. In the transition
period from a mission-supported and directed work to
a completely indigenous church, it may be necessary to
adopt certain temporary measures. We may not be able
to change over completely with one stroke.

In adopting temporary measures, we must not become discouraged with the main plan, nor lose sight of
the goal. We must continue to pray, teach and believe.
*Also we must beware lest temporary measures become
permanent policies.* Our objective must be unalterable,
but the methods may be fluid, to be revised from time
to time to meet the exigencies of changing conditions.
One reason why it may sometimes be necessary to temporarily stop short of our final goal, is to enable our
national brethren to come along with us in our thinking. The very principles of the indigenous church require that they think for themselves, so it is understood
that the steps to be taken should have the general approval of the nationals themselves.[2]

[2]It might be noted here that since mission funds come from
mission sources, it is not within the jurisdiction of the nationals
to determine the amount of foreign funds which may be used in
the work. The missionaries, since they are the ones who are held

TEACH LOCAL CONGREGATIONS

An initial action which might readily obtain the approval of all should be a hold-the-line policy as to the use of foreign funds for the support of national workers. In other words, having taken the wrong road, we will proceed in that direction no further. We will henceforth seek to meet the needs that arise in the work from national sources, without employing additional foreign funds. Following this, steps should be taken to develop local sources for the support of workers which heretofore have been dependent on mission funds. Each organized church should become responsible for the support of its pastor. This means that we teach indigenous principles to the local congregations.

If the churches have not been properly organized with their own official board and pastor, this should be done according to the procedure already explained in chapter 3. After teaching and explaining, we may hold business sessions with the board and with the entire church, urging them to come to some conclusion concerning the support of their pastor. In some cases it may be necessary to give them a little time for study and decision. The date of complete responsibility may be postponed for three to six months. Or we may soften the blow somewhat by reducing the present salary of the worker, perhaps one-third every three months, until he is completely dependent upon the church for support. This last suggestion has its disadvantages, however, since sometimes the church fails to respond until it knows that its pastor is completely dependent upon the members. The plan has been successfully worked out in numerous instances.

responsible, will determine this. Once funds are made available for the work, the nationals may be consulted as to how they may best be used. However, this particular condition, which results from the process of conversion, is abnormal. The necessity of allocating foreign funds for the maintenance of pastors or churches will disappear as the work attains the goal of self-support.

If we have a choice, it is preferable to use foreign funds to temporarily aid the struggling local church with the rent of their building, or in the construction of their church, rather than to help in the matter of the pastor's salary. When we must continue to assist in the matter of the pastor's salary for a time, it is better to pay the money into the local church treasury, thus permitting the pastor to receive the help from the church treasury rather than from the mission directly. This tends to avoid the idea that the worker is supported by the mission. It also makes for a healthier relationship between pastor and congregation.

HELPING A NEEDY WORKER

It is recognized that occasions do arise when it is a duty to succor a needy brother. In such cases, it is not only the duty of the missionary, but of the whole Christian constituency, to help. Why should the missionary alone assume the responsibility of showing Christian charity? Should not the members of the church and neighboring congregations as well respond to the need of a brother in distress? Usually if the matter is brought to their attention, they will gladly help a truly worthy brother. The missionary, as a brother in Christ, may also share in this gift. In such cases of pressing need, it is better to make an outright gift in order to help a worker through the crisis, rather than to promise him a monthly allowance. On the former plan he can thank God for supplying his need and continue on his way in faith, anticipating that God will care for him.

Fourth, the national leaders themselves should have a say as to how money available for the development and the maintenance of the work is to be used. This is particularly true of money that comes from local sources. Such questions as to which evangelist should be chosen for a certain task, and how much help he is to receive while carrying out his commission are questions which the missionary should not decide alone. The executive board should make such decisions. This board should include a sufficient number of nationals so that the voice of the national church can be heard. The missionary thus avoids unfavorable criticism. At least criticisms are less severe when the nationals share this responsibility with the missionary. It is an important step in the right direction when the national brethren are given a voice as to the distribution of funds.

CONVERSION COMPLETED

The final step in converting from a mission-supported work to a self-supporting work is to place the entire responsibility for the *maintenance of the work* on the national churches. For some time afterward, the mission may still share with national churches the tasks of evangelizing new territory, the training of workers, literature publication, etc., but eventually even these responsibilities will be borne by the nationals.

PROCESS OF CONVERSION ILLUSTRATED

To illustrate the general process, I shall relate some of our own experiences as we went through the struggle of changing from a mission-supported work to the indigenous church methods in a field where we served early in our missionary ministry. Certainly I do not present ourselves as models for others to follow. My wife and I were inexperienced in missionary work, but certain factors did favor us. We had a firm conviction that the indigenous principles pointed the way to victory and, since we were the only missionaries of our denomination in the country, we did not have to battle with divided opinions on the part of the missionary staff.

The work on this field was small but not new. Upon arrival, we found four small churches and four workers. Two of these workers were receiving support directly from mission headquarters in the United States since there had been no resident missionary there for a number of years. The other two were new workers who

looked forward to receiving some help as soon as a
missionary might again be stationed on the field. In
the meantime, the workers who were supported gen-
erously helped the two who received no help, giving
them tithes and offerings from their own allowances.

From the very first, we began to place emphasis on
the necessity of the work becoming self-supporting. We
organized the groups that had not been set in order,
encouraging them to become self-governing. We also
endeavored to inspire those converts in the churches
who felt a call to the work of God to step out in faith.
They began to respond to our plea, but did not take
seriously our ideas about the work becoming self-supporting. They thought that it was an idealistic dream
and, that given time, we would begin to dole out mission funds to support the workers as the former missionary had done. All other missionary societies operating in that country were doing the same thing.

The number of volunteers grew until there were
about ten full-time or part-time workers, two of them
supported by funds from the United States and the
others either dependent on what their congregations
could supply, or working part time in order to exist.
The inequality was too apparent. I had determined,
however, not to proceed any farther along the road of
designating mission funds for the support of workers,
for I realized that the indigenous principles presented
the only road to spiritual prosperity for the work. In
the meantime, the workers waited more or less patiently
for me to wake up and give them the help they needed.

One day one of the workers who received support
from the mission, told me of the need of one of the
brethren and dropped a broad hint that it was time to
help him financially. He said, "I just told him to be
patient; you are waiting to see his faithfulness. When
you are sure that he is going to be a good worker, you
will ask for support from the mission for him." So they
nursed the hope that better days would come.

THE CRISIS

Finally after a little more than a year, the crisis occurred. Upon our first visit to the field, with the aid of a more experienced missionary, we had brought the churches together to form a conference. The storm broke at the second anniversary of the conference. I was presiding at a business session when one of the newer workers arose and said, "Brother, my family is suffering. I have several children. I cannot continue in the work unless I can have the promise of regular monthly support." With that he came forward and handed to me his license to preach. Others followed him, one by one, though in a less dramatic manner. With the exception of four, the workers said that they could not continue. One of these four—he received support from the mission—tried to exhort the discontented to faithfulness. The others remained silent.

I lifted my heart to God for guidance. This was the decisive moment. Finally I said something like this: "Brethren, I feel deeply your need and your suffering. I will do all that I can to help you, but I cannot promise a single worker a salary. The support of the work must come from the country itself. Now if the mission has called you to preach, you can place your resignation with the mission. But if you are called of God, it does no good to turn in your resignation to me—you must answer to God. It is not a question between you and me, but between you and God. Are you called of God, or not?" Then I waited with a prayer in my heart.

The brethren were all quiet for several moments. Finally one of the leaders who received no help, asked to say a word. "Brethren, I feel that we have been hasty. I've gone through a lot, as have you. We talk about trusting God, but I wonder if I have ever really trusted God for my support. For my part, I withdraw my resignation and state here that I am going to put God to the test for one year."

Slowly, as God moved on their hearts, the others

stood up, one by one, to say that they would put God
to the test for another year. We didn't keep every
worker, but almost all of them remained with us. So
we entered the new year with renewed strength.

ALL WORKERS ON SAME FOOTING

But the battle was still far from won. I felt strongly
the matter of the financial inequality among the workers, so I wrote a letter to our missionary secretary, asking for counsel. He answered somewhat as follows: "I
believe that we should take away the offerings from the
brethren who now receive designated support. We shall
give them six months time before this becomes effective,
in order for them to make the necessary adjustments.
Then we will place this same amount at your disposal,
so that you can help the brethren as you see the need."

The two brethren concerned were then advised that
they would be receiving offerings from the mission for
only six months more, and that from then on, all
workers would be on the same footing. One of them was
a visiting worker from another Latin American country.
When he found out that he would not receive his offering, he decided to return home. I did not dissuade
him, not because I did not appreciate his labors, but I
realized that we must build of native material, and unless he were willing to take his place with the rest of
the pastors, his presence would not benefit the work.
He returned to his own country and has done a good
work for God there. The other worker took a manly
attitude, making his plans so that within six months he
had a little business going on the side to tide him over
the crisis.

At the end of the six months, the money was sent to
me, as agreed, rather than to the two workers. I shared
with the national leaders of our conference the responsibility for the distribution of these funds. During this
time of transition, I traveled constantly, visiting the
churches and encouraging them to support their own

workers, endeavoring to establish tithing as the scriptural basis for giving to God's work. After some months, the worker who had been deprived of his offering testified as follows: "Brethren, you know that I felt that Brother Hodges had been quite severe with me when he arranged to have my offering taken away after I had served for so many years. But I saw that if I were to prosper, I must needs get busy and build up my church. So I have been working with my people, and now I am proud to say that I am not dependent upon the mission, but I have developed my own church."

NATIONALS VOTE SELF-SUPPORT

A few years later, after God had visited that field with revival and the number of workers had increased to more than twenty, it was my great joy to be with these workers in a conference when the nationals themselves made a motion, and adopted the same, to the effect that *all* funds coming to the field from outside the country were to be used only for Bible school or evangelistic effort. No such funds were to be used for the suport of pastors of established churches. Thus, little by little, the idea had taken hold of them, and they had accepted it as basic and practical.

In that same meeting, one of the leaders was trying to make a point and by way of illustration said, "When Brother Hodges started to preach to us about a self-supporting church on this field, we thought that he was dreaming. We said that it could never be done. But he just kept hammering away, month after month, and now look at us—we, ourselves, have put this motion through. It has come from the workers, not the missionaries, and we are all glad for it."

9

HINDRANCES TO CONVERSION TO INDIGENOUS PRINCIPLES

Many of the well-established missions are making a decided effort to introduce indigenous church principles into their mission work. Lessons dearly learned during World War II convinced many missionaries that the indigenous way is the only way which brings lasting results. Even so, many missions which profess to believe in these principles, as well as many missionaries who pay lip service to them, stop short of taking the necessary steps toward conversion, or "devolution," as the process of turning the reins of government into the hands of the nationals is sometimes called. Why the hesitancy? Let us examine some of the possible reasons.

RELUCTANCE TO SURRENDER AUTHORITY

First, perhaps unconsciously the missionary is reluctant to surrender the prestige and power which his present position affords. The man who is accustomed to having the decisive voice may find it difficult to turn over that authority to others, or to surrender title or position. Similarly, he may hesitate to relinquish his control of the purse strings. He knows that in his hands, money produces activity. It also gives authority to his voice in church matters. Perhaps, without realizing what has taken place, he has come to have more faith in the results he can obtain by his use of money than he has in those results which the Holy Spirit can produce in the heart of the convert. As John Ritchie says,

> So long as the policies [of self-support] are dictated by considerations of convenience, there will be frequent cases in which the immediate advantages of subsidy will induce the missionary to depart from the harder way. . . . The desirability of retaining influence over the congregation by the power of the purse, of keeping hold of a promising worker, of maintaining the status of the group, above all the desire to bind the church to his person and his mission, will seem to commend the wisdom of subsidy to the missionary whose criterion is pragmatic.[1]

LOSS OF POPULAR APPEAL

Second, the presentation of the indigenous church to the home constituency involves the loss of a certain popular financial appeal. The founding of the indigenous church is the primary objective of missionary activity, and should therefore have the highest appeal to well-informed Christians at home. Yet, it is a well-known fact that many Christians respond more readily in their missionary giving to an appeal for projects which are really secondary. The plea to support an orphan child, for example, or help famine sufferers, will bring a ready response. The visible often has more appeal than the invisible, hence many missionaries are tempted to carry on a type of work which makes a better showing at home, and which brings in more financial help.

Third, a sincere desire to show Christian charity by helping the underprivileged and relieving suffering may cause the missionary to cling to procedures that weaken the indigenous church.

HONEST CHRISTIAN CHARITY

The Bible inquires, "Whoso hath this world's good, and seeth his brother have need, and shutteth up his

[1] John Ritchie, *Indigenous Church Principles*, pp. 29-30.

bowels of compassion from him, how dwelleth the love
of God in him?" Then are not missionaries with the resources of rich America behind them, obliged to do
everything in their power to relieve the want of the less
fortunate around them? Are we not to feed the hungry
and clothe the naked for Christ's sake?

One of the factors which make the problem difficult
to analyze is the difference in the standards of living.

It is a recognized fact that there is a great contrast
between the standard of living in the United States
and most countries where foreign missionaries now
work. . . . There is, therefore, the unconscious tempta-
tion on the part of the missionary to feel that he should
try to raise the standard of living of the people to
whom he ministers. The standard of living which he
considers the norm is, of course, that of the United
States of America. This is a false premise. Christian
salvation is not a matter of civilization. It is true that
backward civilizations have been greatly improved by
the influence of the Lord Jesus Christ . . . but this is
a by-product of Christianity and is a historical result
whenever Christ becomes an influence in the hearts of
individuals. This change in the standard of living,
however, should come *through the national* church and
not be imposed by foreign missionaries. Ideally, the
only time financial assistance for an improved standard of living should be given to Christians in foreign
lands is when the standard has been lowered *below
normal* for that area by unusual circumstances (flood,
famine, etc.).

The gospel of salvation is effective in changing any
people on any level of civilization.[2] The duty of the
missionary is not primarily to introduce higher standards of living . . . [but] to preach the gospel and assist
in building the church. . . . Satan is very eager to
throw a smoke-screen or fog around the whole missionary process in an effort to get the missionary and
the new Christians to dissipate their energies in an

[2]For further comment see Paul W. Harrison, "Salvation Independent of Economic Conditions," in Sidney J. W. Clark, *The
Indigenous Church*, p. 1 ff.

effort to change the physical aspects found in the mode of living.[3]

SOCIAL BENEFITS THROUGH THE CHURCH

The reason we are so interested in missions is not only because Christ has commanded us to "go into all the world" but because we have realized the value of a soul. We know it does *not* profit if a man gains the whole world and loses his own soul. For this reason we are interested in evangelism. . . . When, through the Holy Spirit's leadership, this is accomplished, it not only gives peace in the midst of existing conditions, but often also gives an individual a desire to better his social conditions. It would seem that those who hold to indigenous principles are as much in favor of securing the social benefits of the gospel as any other Christian group, with this modification: the supporters of indigenous work believe that these benefits, the care of the widows and orphans, the healing of the sick, the education and training of the Christian constituency, should come *through the church* instead of through the missionary. Initial organizational plans and leadership may come from the missionary but ideally the material support should come from the local church and its environment. This is the indigenous method, the New Testament way. To allow foreign material resources to underwrite these features of the local church program is to weaken the church. It will stunt its growth. . . . Between those who can think and work only for social betterment in foreign lands, and those whose missionary work is only for the salvation of souls, are those who have the concept of saving souls in order that the national Christian church may be established; which, in turn, will become the "salt" of the earth and implement the social blessings of the Christian church. Anything that does not assist in establishing the Church of Christ should be discouraged. *Anything which hinders the development of the Church, no matter how much immediate good it does, should be sacrificed for the slower but more permanent*

[3]"A Study of Indigenous Policies and Procedures," paper of the Conservative Baptist Foreign Missions Society, p. 9.

*good achieved through the establishment of the in-
digenous church.*[4]

CONFUSING THE CONVERTS

By assisting the nationals to better their conditions
with American funds and plans, there is always the
danger of confusing the minds of the nationals as to
what Christianity really is. In the minds of these
Christians, the gospel message, with its emphasis on
salvation, becomes mixed with the material by-products
of the gospel. . . .[5]

It is quite apparent that whether it is in Africa,
South America or in Asia the people react in much the
same way. They begin to expect material help wher-
ever and whenever they can. . . . When we analyze
the psychological results of free drugs, free schooling
and free supplies upon the Christians, we soon find the
"rice Christian" psychology manifesting itself. The
people, being very human, naturally gravitate to the
mission where they can receive these material helps.
When the material help is not forthcoming, then the
individual missionary begins to sense a definite loss in
their interest in his services. Some of these people
being primitive are very frank and remark: "What is
the use of being a Christian if we do not receive these
benefits?" It is then that we begin to realize that
these things which we thought would help the people
have only hindered and confused them. The gospel
message and its intent have been confused with the
benefits which we thought were so essential as an out-
ward expression of our concept of the gospel. . . . The
people have unconsciously joined the group who followed Jesus because they thought He would be King
and provide them with food. . . . Eventually a clear
thinking missionary begins to realize that these benefits must be foregone if he is to get the true message of
salvation and Jesus' purpose in coming to this world
across to these people who have lived in heathen darkness and idolatrous practices.[6]

[4]*Ibid.*, p. 5.
[5]*Ibid.*, p. 6.
[6]*Ibid.*, p. 11.

WANT QUICK RESULTS

Fourth, the very ability and efficiency of the missionary may strangely enough prove to be a hindrance to the development of the church. Impatient to attain certain goals, the missionary may use the direct approach instead of the slower, indirect approach through the nationals. Americans are noted for their ability to get things done. We are psychologically geared to the machine age. "Fast" and "big" are words which occur frequently in our speech. "Within the boundaries of our evangelical standards, anything that will produce results more rapidly is looked upon with favor even though the permanent results may not be as satisfactory as [those] which might be obtained from other methods."[7]

We Americans establish systems and a tempo that are beyond the capacity of the national. These do not fit his nature. He observes the way the missionary does things, and he knows that he cannot do them in that way, so he becomes discouraged. He cannot understand the American system of bookkeeping. He cannot carry through a complicated program that requires the coordination of several diverse activities. Again, the missionary may be a gifted musician and insist on the use of beautiful English hymns. Perhaps under his guidance the converts learn to sing them with a piano accompaniment. When the missionary goes, the converts miss the piano, and their efforts to sing lack luster. Would it not be better to allow them to accompany their hymns on a one-stringed instrument with which they are familiar, one which they could continue to use when the missionary is not present?

Thus the missionary is sometimes too capable for the good of the native church. He does too much and sets too fast a pace. The converts watch him—not without admiration—and decide that since the missionary does things so well, he is the one to do them. Someone has

[7]*Ibid.,* p. 4.

illustrated this point by asking how we would feel if we were placed in the midst of a group of sleight-of-hand performers. Everything that we tried to do for ourselves, such as to dress ourselves, would be done for us by magic in the twinkling of an eye. Certainly we would end up feeling frustrated, bewildered and discouraged, for we have not had training to fit us for that kind of life. Similarly the quick, efficient Americans are like sleight-of-hand performers to the slower nationals. It is futile to try to force them into our pattern; we only discourage them. Rather, the missionary is the one who needs to educate himself and change his ways so that he follows a pattern natural to the nationals. We should not make the pattern of the work so foreign that it requires a foreign education to carry it on.

The missionary, for instance, may be unwilling to wait for a national church to find the resources and make the effort to put up its chapel. He knows that he can appeal to friends at home and receive more in one month than the church will raise in a year. His desire to "have something to show" for his labors may cause him to put to one side the efforts of the nationals and go ahead to put up the building with foreign funds.

Or the missionary may feel that he should continue to fill the pastorate of the church where he resides, because there is no national worker "big enough" for the central church. Better crowds attend when the missionary preaches, and he is somewhat impatient with the slow and easy approach of the national workers. The trouble is that while there seem to be more immediate results through following nonindigenous practices, permanent results are far more discouraging. And permanent results—those which remain after the missionary has gone—are the true test of his labors.

10

RELATIONSHIP OF THE MISSIONARY TO THE INDIGENOUS CHURCH

The adjustment which the missionary is able to make to his environment and the relationship which he maintains with the church that he plants, have no small influence upon the success of his labors. In this chapter we discuss a few of the problems in this connection and then summarize the missionary's proper ministry.

ADJUSTMENT TO ENVIRONMENT

The first problem is that of physical adjustment to the native environment, both in the home and in the general manner of life. Someone has stated that a missionary is "called to cross national and cultural barriers which separate the peoples of this world. He is the 'apostle to the Gentiles,' a calling which necessitates a break with his own people and the adoption of a new home in a strange land. But the mere fact that a person leaves his native land for a foreign shore is no indication that the national and cultural barrier has been crossed. The missionary frequently fails to make the break. He takes America with him. He establishes a small colony within the walls of the mission compound. . . . No effort is made to adopt the ways of the foreign country as we would expect a guest to adjust his life in the home of a friend." A consecrated Christian Indian worker makes this criticism: "It pains us to see that some of our excellent missionaries have so little appeal to the people of India. This is because they live a life out of all proportion to their environment."

Yet, we are here making no plea for the missionary to "go native." We have observed that as a general rule the nationals do expect the American missionary to live on a different economic plane than the poorer nationals can afford. As a matter of fact, whether the national recognizes it or not, it would be almost a physical impossibility for the missionary with his wife and children to adjust to native food and housing conditions. Even under the best conditions possible, the missionaries suffer breakdowns in health because of the diseases common to their new environment and the changes in climate and food. The man of average constitution finds it necessary either to live on a higher scale than the nationals or to discontinue missionary work. Furthermore, it is only fair to the missionary's children to rear them in an atmosphere that will familiarize them a bit with American culture, so that when they return to the homeland they will not be misfits. These reasons are sufficient to explain the necessity of a scale of living for the missionary that would be beyond the reach of the average national.

Nevertheless, the missionary who lives in even the most modest surroundings, according to American standards, must seem, in the eyes of the nationals, to live like a king. They cannot but know that the missionary family spends as much for one day's food as the poor national will spend to feed an equal number of people for nearly a week. And the missionary may nonchalantly spend the equivalent of a day laborer's monthly wage for some item which appears to the national to be a nonessential trinket. Thus missionaries, along with Americans in general, are considered "rich"; and it is useless for a missionary to protest that he is poor, or that a ditchdigger in the United States makes more money than he does.

This discrepancy is a source of vexation in the mind of the national Christian and especially of the national worker, who struggles along with so little. It is also a source of distress to the conscientious missionary. Some such missionaries allow their sympathy to cloud their judgment. They begin to hand out financial gifts to the workers and Christians, thus starting down the road toward the very thing they desire to avoid: a church or worker financially dependent upon the mission. The missionary should remember that with all of his struggles, the worker is doubtless no worse off financially than he was before his conversion. He is likely better off than his own brothers still in heathenism. On the other hand, the missionary should endeavor to live as simply as possible, and make no more show of money than is absolutely necessary. Explaining that articles of equipment such as his refrigerator and car were made possible by sacrificial gifts of friends who desired to help him and his family to live in a difficult climate and aid him in spreading the gospel, may help in giving the national the right perspective.

MODERN EQUIPMENT

What about the use of modern transportation and equipment such as power saws, electric lights and public-address systems? One mission board handles the question in this way:

> Indigenous methods, strictly applied, would rule out these modern factors if they were beyond the mechanical and technological level of the people we are trying to reach. If nationals could not carry on with these modern things without the help of the white man, and if they could not afford to buy these things if they had to be replaced, then there is a doubt as to the advisability of their use. It can just as logically be argued that the using of these modern things increases the effectiveness of the missionary one thousand per cent.

Both arguments are logical and right. This illustration
may throw a bit of light on the problem: A good father
can do a certain job better and faster than his son,
but he lets his son do it in order to teach him how to
do it. He is preparing the son for the day when he
will be on his own. He will not train the son with tools
which the son himself cannot have later in life.

From this illustration we may draw the general conclusion which may answer both logical arguments expressed above: As far as possible on compounds and
stations the missionary should use the transportation
and mechanical developments used by the people. This
is one phase of "reaching them on their own level."
Where the missionary, after prayer and consideration,
feels that the advantages gained by using modern
things more than offset the disadvantages, he should
use them only for personal use and not try to integrate
them into the indigenous church. [Illustration: use a
saw mill and a truck to build, but do not give the saw
and truck to the national church.] . . . Through all
of this it should be kept in mind that spiritual con-
cepts taught [and absorbed] are far more important
and lasting than any material progress made. . . .
Even though the nationals may greatly desire the foreign aid, we must carefully evaluate whether or not it
will weaken the recipients.[1]

A second problem, the financial relationships of the
missionary with the indigenous church and the danger
of the wrong use of foreign funds, has already been
mentioned. What is the legitimate use of foreign funds
in missionary work, outside of the personal support and
expenses of the missionary himself?

Of course missionaries and missions should not be
niggardly. There is a wise and loving use of money
which opens the very gates of Heaven to many a soul.
But on mission fields, as at home, it is easy to . . .
[misinterpret] a warm, sacrificial love of Christ and
love for the people which would pour itself out for
them without thought of remuneration, . . . [and

[1] "A Study of Indigenous Policies and Procedures," paper of
the Conservative Baptist Foreign Missions Society, p. 8.

respond with] a calculating, selfish attitude which demands so much pay for so much work. Indeed, every missionary society at home ought to make sure that its money is not used to the detriment of that which it would build up.[2]

And this from *The Independent Board Bulletin:*

Although a missionary must be extremely careful in the use of money, nevertheless he must show the people that it has cost him something to bring the gospel to them. Financial gifts rarely impress native Christians as involving any real sacrifice. On many fields the people in general think that all foreigners, Americans especially, are rich, and Christians share these views. It is in this connection that actual physical hardship and suffering speak to foreign peoples more eloquently than does the sacrifice of position, loved ones or native land. Indeed, I have seen a pair of blistered feet do more for the advancement of the gospel than had gifts of hundreds of dollars by the missionary who owned those feet.

This principle carries all the way through. Though one may deny a plea for funds with which to build a church, if he will sit down and help a congregation to figure out ways and means of building that church, if he will help them with his own hands, the people will see that he is actually giving in a way that costs. *To sum it up, one might say that the missionary should do only those things which the young church is unable to do for itself, not the things it is unwilling to do. And he should make certain that he does not decide too quickly, too unwisely, that a church is actually unable to do any task whatever that faces it.*

As a general policy, foreign funds may best be invested in those aspects of the work that are beyond the reach of the local churches, that serve to advance the work in the *district*, rather than the local church. Such use of foreign money can be a blessing *as long as we do not build in dependence upon those funds, nor substitute the effort of the nationals with that of our own,*

[2]*Ibid.*

and so cripple initiative. We are to help the churches
do things, not do things for them.[3]

A project which would hasten the evangelization of
a new district could well merit the wise investment of
foreign funds. In my opinion, a Bible school for the
training of national workers is one project where foreign funds may really be of help. Yet those funds
should not be used in such a way as to cause the student and churches to expect the mission to carry the
financial burden for them. Investment in a tract of
land in order to raise food for the Bible school, under
the supervision of the national church, could well pay
rich dividends, and help to make the Bible school self-
supporting. Always the missionary must think in terms
of a self-supporting work. He should initiate each department of the work in such a manner that the nation-

---

[3]It has at times been deemed advisable to make an exception
to the general rule that no help from foreign funds should be
given for the construction of the local church building. In many
of the large cities of the world the price of land is so high that
it would seem to put a suitable location beyond the reach of the
local congregation. It has been felt that it is legitimate to give
help to the church in getting a foothold in large cities. Sometimes help is given for the purchase of the land with the responsibility left to the local church to raise funds for the building.
Again, one missionary society which follows indigenous church
principles in establishing churches agrees to give one-third of the
amount of the entire project if the national church will raise
another third and advance the final third as a loan to be paid
back by the church. In our experience, the practice of making a
loan available to a national has proved generally satisfactory.
Loans have been faithfully repaid and the local congregation
maintains a good sense of responsibility.

Care must be taken, however, that the exception does not
become the rule. It should be pointed out also that the congregation of the indigenous churches in Brazil and Chile have
erected very fine edifices, in some cases costing hundreds of
thousands of dollars. This has been done completely independently of foreign funds and by the sacrifice of the people themselves. Ordinarily the congregations are made up of people of
comparatively low income, so it would not be proper to say that
it is impossible for the indigenous church to erect suitable buildings, even in the large cities.

als can carry on after he has gone. He should refrain from starting anything that the nationals themselves cannot maintain after the withdrawal of the missionary and his funds.

MISSIONARY'S MINISTRY SUMMARIZED

It is now in order that we should summarize the missionary's *ministry* to the indigenous church:

1. The missionary is primarily a planter of churches. This work includes two phases: evangelizing the unconverted, and teaching the converts, which in turn, includes the training of national workers and leaders.

2. The missionary is a temporary factor in any local area, and he should build the church in such a way that it will be able to continue after he has gone. He should not center the work in himself or in the mission, but make the church the center.

3. Since the missionary is a temporary factor, he should not allow himself to become bogged down with the routine of maintaining the work, but seek to occupy new fields. He cannot expect every detail of evangelism and organization to be worked out perfectly before he relinquishes the direct oversight.

4. If the missionary finds an indigenous work already under way in his area, either the product of spontaneous national effort or the fruit of missionary labors, he must be extremely careful not to adopt measures that will choke it out. Missionaries are usually eager to get such works "in hand" (which means "under mission control"), and in doing so they can easily stifle them. The missionary may be tempted to pay a salary to the leader of the indigenous work. Later he may find the converts doing only a small part, with pay, in comparison to what they previously did without his financial assistance.

5. The missionary should refuse to occupy a position that a national can fill. He should avoid becoming tied down to a local pastorate, but keep free for the work of extension. He should count it a triumph when he is

able to place upon the shoulders of national leaders the responsibilities which he has been carrying.

6. The missionary should not be jealous of his own authority or position, but be willing for others to take the lead. He should earn his position of leadership in the national church on the merits of his character and ministry. He must not feel that he merits a position of authority because he is a missionary. If the national church has produced leaders who can fill the offices in the work, the missionary should not object to their taking office; he should insist that they do so. The missionary's spiritual ministry will always provide him his proper place in the body of Christ, whether he holds an office or not.

TIME OF WITHDRAWAL

7. There is undoubtedly a danger that the missionary may withdraw too soon from the work. But there is also the danger that he may fail to withdraw at the proper time. A withdrawal is premature when a missionary leaves the field before he has provided for the teaching and leadership that are vital to the indigenous church. A church left without leaders and teachers is subject to the dangers of error and fanaticism. Converts may lapse back into heathenism and the church disintegrate. These dangers can be avoided by following the Pauline example. He did not leave the churches he founded without instruction or leadership. Thus, it is not enough that the missionary gather a group of converts; they must be incorporated into a church under the guidance of the Holy Spirit.

Failure to withdraw at the proper time breeds discontent and dwarfs the national Christian leadership. It also holds the missionary in that one district when he could move on to a fruitful pioneer ministry.

After the missionary has turned over the leadership of the national church to its own leaders, he may still serve that church by placing himself at its disposal. He may be asked to help in the Bible school with the training of national workers; or it may be desired that he push an aggressive evangelization program in some unevangelized area of the district. At the same time he will strengthen the new administration with his counsel. When a national leadership has been developed sufficiently to guide the churches; when there are national brethren prepared to teach new workers in the Bible school; and when a progressive evangelism has been initiated in the main areas of the district; then the missionary's work in that district is finished. He can with a grateful heart move on into a neighboring district, or transfer to a new field, to begin once more his unique ministry as a planter of churches.

The Missionary's Spiritual Leadership

In no other aspect will the missionary influence the indigenous church as he will in the matter of spiritual leadership. Above everything else, he must be a spiritual example to his converts and to the workers, a man who can prevail with God and prepare the way for the moving of the Holy Spirit. It is sad, then, when national converts and Christians outstrip the missionary in spiritual vision. They look to the missionary not merely for his organizational ability and Bible knowledge, but for leadership and inspiration. Sometimes they have not found these qualities in the missionary and have had to go on without him. Above all else, let the missionary maintain his standing as a "man of God." With this relationship maintained, all other relationships will be made easy.

11

PENTECOST AND INDIGENOUS METHODS

Spiritual awakenings and revivals can be lost through lack of proper methods for harnessing these movements and conserving their results. This is one reason why indigenous methods are so important. A great revival can die out or become ineffective if it is not channeled in a scriptural course toward New Testament goals. Furthermore, even the best methods will produce nothing unless accompanied by the work of the Holy Spirit. What gasoline and spark are to the mechanism of a well-tuned motor, spiritual power is to indigenous church methods, for two essential factors combine to make the church a going concern. The mechanics of a successful church on the mission field are the New Testament methods; the dynamics are the power and ministries of the Holy Spirit. Either factor alone is incomplete and inadequate.

This perhaps explains why we have reports from some sections that indigenous methods have been tried but, after reaching a certain stage, the work failed to make progress. The workers, they say, lacked initiative and the churches barely held their own. Some have used this as an argument against the indigenous method. They claim that the nationals simply are not up to an aggressive program; that left to themselves they lapse into inertia; and that a missionary must constantly be on hand to inspire and direct if the church is to make progress. The trouble will not be found in the indigenous methods, for these are the New Testament methods. The difficulty may be that the indigenous methods have been *only partially or imperfectly applied*; or on the other hand, having been applied, *they have not been accompanied by New Testament power*. New Testament Christians received such an enduement of power, such an inflow of divine life, that their doubts, fears and inertia were swept aside. They "went everywhere" testifying of the resurrection of Christ. Though we may have perfectly set up the "mechanism" of an indigenous church, if it lacks the divine "combustible" of the Holy Spirit's power, it will still be ineffective.

Many have witnessed the miracle of transformation which the presence of the Holy Spirit produces in a national church. They have seen lethargic and reluctant workers transformed into zealous witnesses, willing to launch out into new towns and villages without any promise of support. Suspicious, sensitive and squabbling believers have been melted together by divine love and have become a powerful force for the kingdom of God.

Producing the Power

To be successful in the indigenous church ministry, the missionary must not only be able to teach and initiate the converts in right methods, but also be able to introduce them into the realm of the Holy Spirit's workings. New Testament methods coupled with New Testament power is the answer to the present-day problems of our mission fields. Let the missionaries of each field gather together to pray until there comes from heaven the spiritual power necessary for an awakening according to the apostolic pattern. Let them initiate the converts also into this prayer ministry for revival. Let missionaries and nationals not only preach a gospel of power, but pray until they themselves catch the flame in their own hearts. It is impossible to expend more energy than we receive from our source.

We must give time, both individually and collectively, to this most important of all ministries.

To pray until God's blessings are poured out upon the district of his labors, to channel those blessings by New Testament methods toward the founding of a vigorous national church—this is the ministry which justifies the presence of the missionary on the foreign soil and gives him a rightful claim to the noble title of "Church Builder."

Jesus said: "I will build my church; and the gates of hell shall not prevail against it" (Matt. 16:18).

"And they went forth, and preached every where, the Lord working with them, and confirming the word with signs following" (Mark 16:20).

BIBLIOGRAPHY

Allen, Roland. *Missionary Methods: St. Paul's or Ours?* London: World Dominion, 1930.

Brown, A. J. *The Foreign Missionary.* New York: Revell, 1907.

Cooksey, J. J. *The Land of the Vanished Church.* London: World Dominion, n.d.

Harrison, Paul W. "Salvation Independent of Economic Conditions" in Sidney J. W. Clark, *The Indigenous Church.* London: World Dominion, 1928.

Kane, Herbert J. *Twofold Growth.* Philadelphia: China Inland Mission, 1947.

McLeish, Alexander. "The Effective Missionary" in Sidney J. W. Clark, *The Indigenous Church.* London: World Dominion, 1928.

Ritchie, John. *Indigenous Church Principles in Theory and Practice.* New York: Revell, 1946.

"A Study of Indigenous Policies and Procedures." Paper of the Conservative Baptist Foreign Mission Society.

Upton, George R. Article in *Indian Witness,* periodical of Methodist Publishing House, Lucknow, North India.